GETTING
There

An Exposition Based on the Word of God and Divine Directives

"Seek ye the Lord while He may be found, call ye upon Him while He is near." Is. 55:6.

Copyright ©2024 Felicia Eziuka
All rights reserved.
ISBN 978-1-913455-48-4
First published in 2010
No part of this book shall be reproduced or transmitted in any form or by any means, electronic or mechanical, including photocopying, recording, or by any information retrieval system without prior written permission of the author and publisher.
Published by Scribblecity Publications United Kingdom.
Printed in Great Britain.
Although every precaution has been taken in the preparation of this book, the publisher and author assume no responsibility for errors or omissions. Neither is any liability assumed for damages resulting from the use of this information contained herein.
Scriptures taken from the Holy Bible, New International Version®, NIV®. Copyright © 1973, 1978, 1984, 2011 by Biblica, Inc.™ Used by permission of Zondervan. All rights reserved worldwide. www.zondervan.com The "NIV" and "New International Version" are trademarks registered in the United States Patent and Trademark Office by Biblica, Inc.™
Scripture quotations are from The ESV® Bible (The Holy Bible, English Standard Version®), © 2001 by Crossway, a publishing ministry of Good News Publishers. Used by permission. All rights reserved
Scripture quotations marked (NLT) are taken from the Holy Bible, New Living Translation, copyright © 1996, 2004, 2015 by Tyndale House Foundation. Used by permission of Tyndale House Publishers, Inc., Carol Stream, Illinois 60188. All rights reserved.
Scripture taken from the New King James Version®. Copyright © 1982 by Thomas Nelson. Used by permission. All rights reserved.

Dedication

This book is devoted to the tireless, faithful and loving service of the Holy Spirit in the world since the day of Pentecost.

Acknowledgements

I Hereby Acknowledge with thanks, the help of those who made the writing of this book possible, through advice and encouragement. I also appreciate the contribution of my youngest born, who provided a large supply of literature for my work. May God bless you all in Jesus Name.

Contents

Introduction		12
Chapter One	A Brief Summary of Some Different Ways of Getting There	18
Chapter Two	Be Prepared	21
Chapter Three	Christlikeness	29
Chapter Four	By Prayers	39
Chapter Five	By Righteousness	49
Chapter Six	By The Word	58
Chapter Seven	By Living His Love	62
Chapter Eight	By His Humility	73
Chapter Nine	Separation Unto God	82
Chapter Ten	Through Endurance	92
Chapter Eleven	The Way Of Joy	102
Chapter Twelve	Hidden Errors In Believer's Lives	109
Chapter Thirteen	The Spirit Of Backwardness	121
Chapter Fourteen	The Holy Spirit	133
Chapter Fifteen	Scriptural Negligence	136
Chapter Sixteen	Is There A Compromise?	141

Chapter Seventeen	Christlike Woman.	152
Chapter Eighteen	The Rewards Of The Kingdom	169
Chapter Nineteen	The Self-Imposed Curse	178
Chapter Twenty	Conclusion	180

— **INTRODUCTION** —

This writing is closely supported by quotations from the Bible because of the seriousness of the topic. Getting there is making the Kingdom, which is getting to the likeness of the image of Christ while on this earth. Salvation will be consummated at the arrival of Christ, and the Bible is very explicit on the requirements for making Heaven. This book analyses some of the problems that one encounters in the process of getting there and advises, through the Word, on how to overcome them. The writer uses as examples the divine advice she received on several occasions she had experienced problems. These directives are also scriptural. Divine admonitions and corrections are to be shared as it helps others as they witness how other believers overcame weaknesses, it brings hope and guidance to grow in faith. The book starts with a discussion on the location of the Kingdom life. Man's greatest fear is of death, and the way out of that fear and death is through the blood of the Cross. As of today, Christ is still pleadingly offering man everlasting life through Salvation. This is the way of escape from death and Hell which God spent centuries to carefully work out. Jon. 3:1-7; Isa. 35:8-10.

Christ preached on how to contend with and take authority over the contrary powers, both spiritual and physical, operating here on earth. Eph. 6:10-18. The heart of man is the battleground for the Kingdom and Jesus is the model of instructions to be followed. Having won the victory at the Cross He made grace possible, and gave us the promise of God the Father to help us achieve salvation. Gal. 3:13-15.
It can be said that getting there becomes a matter of living life without sin on this earth. According to this view Heaven can be considered a temporary place of sojourn for saints. He came to restore men as kings and rulers in the Kingdom. Acts 1:6. His disciples asked Him when He would restore the Kingdom to Israel. He replied that it was not for them to know the times and seasons. It can also be said that that was why in Math. 6:10. Jesus taught man to

pray, "Thy Kingdom come. Thy will be done on earth as it is in heaven."

The other line of thought is that Heaven is the final place of abode for saints. Believers who live a holy life will go on rapture with Christ to Heaven; and the tribulation saints will join them there. Christ has prepared enough mansions there. It is believed that it was also the reason why Christ told His disciples in Jon. 14:2 that in His Father's house there were many mansions, and that if it were not so, He would not say so. Whichever view one decides to take, the fact remains that man has to attain Christlike nature because of the finished work at Calvary. In the New Testament, God wants to dwell in the hearts of His people through the Holy Spirit, Who will do the work of sanctification and the renewal of the mind. The Holy Spirit as the Spirit of Truth operates through the Word.

In the book of Heb. 8:10, God said, "I will put My laws into their minds and write them in their hearts, and I will be their God, and they shall be My people." Through the Holy Spirit the Messianic anointing of Jesus will be poured on believers.

Since this age is the last stage of spiritual and moral decay, according to the prophecy in 2 Tim. 3:1-9, God in Christ is still labouring to rescue as many as He can; although He has set a date known to Him alone, when Christ would arrive to consummate salvation on this earth. This book discusses the challenges in the lives of humans responsible for the decay.

The comforting assurance of God's words to Zerubbabel in the book of Zech. 4:6 confirms the central truth of the way to the Kingdom. It says: "Not by might nor by power but by My Spirit, says the Lord of hosts." Reliance on the power of the Holy Spirit is very important. Ps. 32:8 says, "I will instruct thee and teach thee in the way which thou shalt go, I will guide thee with my eye." This is the Holy Spirit teaching and leading the believer on the path of righteousness. Rom. 8:14 reads, "For as many as are led by the Spirit of God, they are the sons of God." This is a revelation of those who are recognised as sons of God. He is the only one who can change the deceitful heart of man and lead him blameless to GOD. Walking in His fruits means walking in grace. His help is indispensable. Only Christ can baptise with the Holy Spirit.

Introduction

The scriptural word "strive" is used to illustrate the difficulties one has to overcome in this journey. The issue of getting to our heavenly destination should not be conceived as an easy journey, but through His mercy. God provided incentives and comfort in order to make the journey easier. Ps. 94:18-19. This encouragement has informed my decision to write on this topic. That a writer can deal with this sensitive topic is not to assume that she is doing very well on "this way". As a matter of fact, she is still striving to navigate her way like other people, by the grace of God.

In Isa. 35:8-10, the scripture refers to "this way" as a highway and reads: "And a highway shall be there, and a way. And it shall be called the highway of holiness. The unclean shall not pass over it, but it shall be for those, the wayfaring men though fools, shall not err there in… nor any ravenous beast shall go therein. It shall not be found there. But the redeemed shall walk there. And the ransomed of the Lord shall return, and come to Zion with singing. With everlasting joy upon their heads. And shall obtain joy and gladness. And sorrow and sighing shall flee away."

Those who are justified by Christ and continue in holiness, looking forward to the hope He provided, not to the discomfort, despite temptations will walk on this road until they get there. It is for all who would believe in the finished work at the Cross and are serious about making Heaven.

What Is This Way?

It is the way of Christ (Phil. 1:29), to suffer with Him (Jon. 14:15), all that Jesus stands for; of the Word (Jon. 8:51); the way of love, by belief and choice, not by circumstances (Jon. 14:15); of prayers (1 Thess. 5:17), of faith, childlike in faith and trusting (Math.19:14); of humility (1 Pet.5:5); of obedience (Jon. 14:15.); of long suffering and endurance (Gal. 6:7); and the way of holiness (1 Pet. 1:16).

Neither one nor two nor three of these ways will get one there. One must strive to walk collectively on all of them and more by the grace of God. We strive to live righteously, because the price for those sins have been paid for by Christ. There is no need to commit them anymore. All we have to do is focus on Christ as a model and obey the Holy Spirit. In the believer's identification with Christ and His characteristics, which is also that of God, he is living the life of Christ by faith. Salvation without holiness is unscriptural. The Holy Spirit, Who is the power of God, will pour out his spiritual resources to make the walk to the kingdom possible.

Chapter One

— A BRIEF SUMMARY —

Jesus is the Way, the only way to salvation. He is also the Word. Jon. 1:1. A divine voice once said to me, "Through the Word you will access heaven." Jon. 8:51. His heart of love and sacrifice was perceived in His lifestyle which He left as a legacy for man to learn and emulate.

The scripture in Acts 1:1 tells us that Jesus began both to do and to teach in His ministry. Within the realm of to do is incorporated the pattern of the life He lived. Our lifestyles should speak for us more than our mouths. Sometimes our words are not the true indication of our hearts. In Jon. 14:6 the scripture tells us that Jesus is the Truth, the Way and the Life. It is our belief in this truth that will set us free from the bondage of sin and make it possible for us to get to the

Kingdom blameless. He is the truth (Jon. 8:32) about God and the Word. He is also that everlasting life He secured for man at the Cross (Rom. 8:2). He made salvation possible through obedience to God and also wants us to make it possible in our lives by following Him in obedience.

The key requirements to be like Christ are faith, love, obedience and humility. Christ taught us that the purpose of the gift of grace is to enable us to live holy lives without repeatedly falling into sin. Since the price for the sin in man has been paid for, there is no need to sin anymore. If we try to bring those sins back, as believers our chances of eventually making salvation will be seriously limited. Some may have to pay with their blood in the end. Sin demands the blood of the sinner. We and God have a common enemy, and that enemy is sin.

Faith is the strength of God that we need in order to defeat sin. It is reflected in the way we think, speak and act. Without works faith will remain dead within the individual, and without a born again heart faith will remain static. It is the fulfilment of God's instructions to man. As we speak the Word of faith on a particular problem, and base our faith on His power to overcome, He will begin to work on it. Rom. 14:23 states that anything not proceeding from faith is considered sinful.

Love, the divine agape love of God, is the key characteristic of God and also of Christ. It is responding to provocations with tolerance and goodness. It is an act of sacrificial kindness. It is based on grace, not on circumstances like the love of man that asks: "What do I stand to gain from this?" God is perfected in love. Jon. 3:16; 15:13. Anything done in love hardly fails. 1 Cor. 13:8. Any reprimand given out of love touches the heart, unlike the one administered in anger, which can stir up resentment. It is advisable and more rewarding to discipline, evangelise and minister out of love. Spiritually mature leaders lead and serve in love. Our lives should centre on the need to extend the love of God to others. This may be through service, blessing, advice, encouragement, smile, brief prayer, etc.

All believers should make fervent and constant prayers an inevitable part of their lives. There is an urgent need, especially at this end time, to reach out and hold on to God through prayers. Aggressive spiritual conflict through prayers is needed in order to break through the violence of the warfare for the Kingdom. Math. 11:12.

Chapter Two

— PREPARE —

"Prepare the way of the Lord, make His paths straight." Mk.1:3

Heaven is the last place that you can walk into without the necessary preparation. This is because the purpose is to meet with the Lord's judgement and render account of one's life on this earth. The preparation requires a life time concentration, seriousness and a spiritual approach. It is rejecting things of the flesh in Gal. 5:19-21, coming into conflict with the ways of the world, and living according to the fruits of the Spirit in Gal. 5:22-23.

In Ex. 19:10-15, when God asked Moses to prepare the Israelites for a meeting He scheduled for them, He mandated him to ensure that adequate preparation was made before they came. He Himself detailed the

preparations.
- They were to purify themselves.
- They were to wash their clothes.
- They were to prepare themselves spiritually.
- They were to keep away from any sexual practices.
- They were to keep away from the mountain. If anyone touched it, that person would die.

All these preparations were to make sure that nothing was standing between Him and them. You can call the preparation for the second coming of Christ a life, or death preparation. Man is supposed to prepare for the second coming of Jesus Christ and follow seriously the Words of the Scriptures, which is the gospel of the Kingdom he left for the Church. Moses was one of the prophets who prophesied the first coming of Christ. He was quoted in the book of Acts 3:22-23 as saying: "The Lord God will raise up for you a Prophet like unto me of your brethren; Him shall ye hear in all things whatsoever He shall say unto you. And it shall come to pass that every soul that shall not hear that Prophet, shall be destroyed among the people." He was talking of Jesus, Who came to reveal to man the right way to prepare for the Kingdom. In this chapter some areas where preparation is needed will be briefly discussed.

Repentance

As sin is the common enemy of everyone so the remission of sin that leads to everlasting life is the greatest need of man. This comes as a result of genuine repentance (feeling sorry for the sin, confessing it, turning away from it and not making reference to it). It leads to a reconciliation between God and man. Isa. 59:2. God is always willing to forgive, and this should serve as an encouragement. 1 Jon.1:8-9, Without repentance one is an eternal enemy of God. Our present level of holiness mirrors the genuineness of our repentance.

Some people on hearing the gospel repent immediately. Among this group may belong,

1. Those who have a good Christian background,

2. Those who have come to the realisation of what salvation means,

3. Those who have become too frightened of God to do otherwise,

4. Those who have received divine healing from terminal diseases or delivered from near threat of death, accident, etc.

5. Those who are escaping from occult entanglement and now fully convinced that Christ is the only way to live. This

last group are the ones who according to Heb. 2:15 through fear of death were all their lifetime subject to bondage.

6. Then you have the Paul type who had perceived Christianity as a threat to their established form of religion. This group may need an encounter with the Holy Spirit or Jesus Christ.

A testimony was given of somebody who came regularly to the Church and was receiving prayers for financial breakthrough. Suddenly she stopped coming. Somebody who ran into her much later tried to find out why she was not coming again. She replied that there was no need to come again because she had received her breakthrough. This type of repentance does not lead to salvation.

Repentance can be partial or complete. Partial repentance means that some sins are repented of while others are not. A genuine heartfelt repentance is not just shedding a lot of tears and feeling sorry when sin is being committed and then going back to that sin again. I am sure that we all have experienced such before. True repentance also requires faith and obedience. Faith motivates obedience.

Repentance is a gift of grace given to us by God. The Holy Spirit imparted it on those with willing hearts. Some people in the world who have missed its relevance ignore it while some perceive it as an act of cowardice. This can mean that the individual has rejected the saving grace of the blood of Jesus. Since Jesus cannot die a second time, it means that the sins of that individual will forever cling to him or her and lead to final damnation. Ezek. 18:4b. Rom. 6:23.

Partial repentance can be a result of the following:

- Lack of the fear and sufficient knowledge of God. Ps. 19:9
- Lack of faith in particular areas of problems. Rom. 2 Cor. 5:7
- Ignorance and incomplete knowledge of the Word. Hos. 4:6
- Influence of evil foundation and hidden covenants. 1 Cor. 3:11
- A belief that nobody can achieve complete righteousness.
- Disbelief in the reality of heaven and hell. Lk. 12:5
- The pull of the flesh and the love of self. Jon. 3:6
- Love of the world and a fear that their world pattern of behaviour will have to be sacrificed. 1 Jon. 2:15.
- Trading one sin for another. 1 Chr. 28:7
- The influence of bad friends. 1 Cor. 15:33

- 1 Jon. 3:8 reads: "He that committeth sin is of the devil; for the devil sinneth from the beginning.

Some Benefits of Living a Righteous life

- Because our God and Creator mandated us to be like Him. Heb. 12:14
- We shall inherit eternal life in the end. Matt. 25:46
- Jesus has destroyed sin at the Cross for us. Col. 2:14-15
- We shall be blessed in the world beyond. Ps. 1:1
- Have peace with God and avoid hell. Is. 26:3
- We shall live a good legacy for our children. 1 Jon. 3:10
- Will experience answered prayers.
- Able to draw people convincingly to Christ. Gal. 6:2
- Be in a position to repossess our possessions. Obad. 1:17
- Will miss hellfire. Matt. 5:22
- Live out our sanctification. 1 Pet. 3:15
- Will not backslide. Jer. 2:9
- Will enjoy divine health. Mal. 4:2
- Be protected by God. Ps. 23:4
- Be able to live in the divine love of God with our neighbours.

A lot depends on what one is trying to repossess. If, for example, you came from an idolatrous background into the fold of Christ, and have lost all your inheritance there, and are therefore asking for a restoration, you have to be careful because the scriptural concept of restoration may not apply here. What you are asking for may be that the defiled things from an idolatrous place will be returned to you. 2 Cor. 6:17b reads, "…and touch not the unclean thing and I will receive you." We ask God to give us His own. Pro. 10:22 states, "The blessing of God makes rich and He adds no sorrow to it." If you continue to ask for what was stolen and is defiled, it may seem as if you desire to go back. It may even mean that He allowed those things to go because they were defiled.

This means that once you are consciously in possession of an unclean thing, you are on hold until you get rid of it. Remember Achan. Josh. 7:1-25. With regards to an inheritance, one has to be careful of what they are inheriting because curses may be passed from one generation to the other through it.

Repentance is a gift of grace given to us by God. It heals human relationships and helps people practise the divine love of God. The Holy Spirit imparts this grace on those with willing hearts.

Our models of genuine repentance are Peter, Math. 26:75, David, 2 Sam. 12:13, and Paul, 1 Tim.1:13. Restitution is as a result of repentance and confirms the genuineness of the heart. Most Churches do open cooperate repentance. This may be as a result of growth in faith. In a Church where I spent my formative years as a minister of God, the General Overseer of the Church would stand in front of the Church and ask all those who committed adultery, fornication and related sins to come out for a confession before God so that prayers can be said for them and their sins forgiven. There may be a brief silence, then they will start coming out. Some covering their faces and some running. There were always many people. They would kneel down and confess their sins quietly before God and the Overseer would pray for them and advise them not to go back to that sin again. Nobody looked down on them but admired their honesty and fear of God. Whenever such a call was made in that Church, many always came out to repent. Sin originally came into man through pride. Gen. 3:5. It usually lives through humility

Chapter Three
— CHRISTLIKENESS —

"Till we all come to the unity of the faith and of the knowledge of the Son of God to a perfect man to the measure of the stature of the fullness of Christ." Eph.4:13

It is likely that we shall be judged by how like Christ we are; how we live out the grace He left for us. We know that grace operates in righteousness and Jesus is the righteousness of God. For this righteousness to be possible, we need to base our faith in Christ and live like Him. Christlikeness can only be achieved through the spiritual renewal of a man's heart by the Holy Spirit.

The Church in Sardis had a good reputation that they were vibrant and alive. When Christ took a look at it, He said, "I know your works, that you have a name, that you are alive, but you are dead." Apart from a few who had not defiled themselves, Jesus could not really perceive His

Christlikeness in their hearts. He knew that sometimes behaviour is not a true reflection of what is in the heart.

Paul said in 1 Cor. 15:10: "But by the grace of God, I am what I am today." He judged his own standard by that of God and attributed the benefits to God alone. This is Christlikeness.

Jesus said in Jon. 9:5: "As long as I am in the world, I am the Light of the world. "This is the Light of life. Christlikeness is to follow this light of His gospel into the righteousness of Christ, which is that of God. Matt. 5:14 reads: "You are the light of the world." In verse 16, He went on to say, "Let your light so shine before men, that they may see your good works and glorify your Father Which is in Heaven." In other words, as we move into the world let that light of the gospel influence people for good. If Christ is the Light, then we have to reflect that light in the way He thought, lived and behaved.

If the Light of Christ influenced people, then our own light should influence others too. If Christ does only good works, then we have to do only that too. Christlikeness is the replica of Acts 17:28, which reads, "In Him we live, move and have our being." We need to have His nature in order to pray and challenge the enemy confidently in His Name.

The process of becoming like Christ may take a long or short time depending on the particular circumstances of the individual. The Holy Spirit is patiently training believers to be like Christ and the training will end when we leave this world. This was one reason why Christ hung on the Cross for us according to Gal. 3:14: "...that we might receive the promise of the Spirit through faith."

The first step of salvation is not the end of the road. It is an open door that will lead to Christlikeness. God values this Christlikeness more than any other attainment. It may appear as if this may be a major reason why certain requests are withheld for a while in order to allow a transformation into the image of Christ. Our minds and attitudes have to show that they are undergoing some change. First, we have to show that the fruits of the Spirit are evidenced in our lives (Gal. 5:22-23), which fruits are Christlike themselves. Christ's pattern of life and ministry is the model to emulate. He was obedient to His parents and was already teaching in the Synagogue at the age of twelve. Lk. 2:42-52. He fasted for forty days and forty nights in the wilderness just before His ministry took off. At the completion of this fast, instead of immediate blessings, Satan emerged to tempt the one through Whom the whole universe was created. Matt. 4:1-11. This is the same pattern of behaviour which Satan extends towards believer's today. The moment you complete a serious fast, even before you have time to wait in expectation for that breakthrough, you may encounter another spiritual attack, signifying that the evil one is enraged at the impending success of your fasting. 1 Pet. 5:8 reads: "Be sober, be vigilant, because your adversary the devil walks about like a roaring lion, seeking whom he may devour." Satan could not touch Christ because he, Satan, had nothing in Him. Likewise, Satan cannot really hurt any believer who has put on Christ as a garment.

Every believing Christian passes through a wilderness experience. It is a period of great temptation, suffering and humiliation in one's life that has no definite period of time. Some people through the grace of God survive this period, while some fail spiritually because of the pressure of discouragement as a result of not being seriously Christlike in their lives. Six hundred thousand fighting men, about 2.5 million Israelites in all, went on the wilderness journey. Only Caleb and Joshua, and the offspring of the others, entered the promised land. Disobedience and lack of faith and endurance might have contributed to this.

In some cases, if one is passing through a wilderness experience, it may seem as if the more you fast and pray, the more the problem would seem to persist. This is not unusual. In order to succeed one may require more prayers, faith, endurance and obedience. Satan cherishes this period because he uses it to discredit many who are not strong in faith. Emerging successful from there does not mean that you can now make Heaven. It will certainly make it easier because of the Christlike qualities you learnt through suffering and obedience. One still needs continuity in order to succeed.

A very close relative of mine was passing through a wilderness experience. Having exhausted myself in all the prayers I could come up with, without the problems getting better, I asked the Lord what was happening to that life. He replied that the person was going through a wilderness experience. Pray that your own experience would be gradual and successful not tempestuous and prolonged. Obedience to the word also has a lot to do with this. The scripture in Phil. 1:29 states that growth in the Lord will only come through suffering.

Jesus operated a very successful ministry here on earth, serving the needs of the oppressed, the poor, the sick and those in bondage. In Jon. 14:27 He said: "Peace I leave with you; My peace I give unto you. Not as the world giveth give I unto you." When you lay all your burden on Him and look forward to the expected joy set for you in the end, you are more likely to experience His peace and rest. Pray that the Holy Spirit will impart the nature of Christ in you.

It is necessary to develop the discipline of spending enough time concentrating on His ways instead of on the distractions that draw our attention away from Him.

The Heart of Christ

A deeply felt, heartbroken, humble repentance that leads to the remission of sins is Christlike. The heart can be said to be the most important area where preparation for heaven needs to be made. This is because anything that enters into it will be reflected in the way one speaks and acts. In Jer. 17:9-10 God said: "The heart is deceitful above all things, and desperately wicked. Who can know it? I the Lord search the heart." This may be one of the reasons why He said in Deut. 4:29 that you will find Him when you seek Him with all your heart. We must strive to come to God with all righteousness of the heart. A troubled heart that is filled with unsettled problems may give rise to doubt and unbelief. This means that the mind may not be able to receive the spiritual things of God from the Holy Spirit. Its renewal becomes difficult. This is a threat to salvation. The Holy Spirit prefers a faithful and loving heart to operate in. According to Pro. 15:18, an upright heart studies to answer.

The undisciplined heart that lets out thoughtless words is not Christlike. When it appeared as if I was letting out a lot years back, a divine voice said to me, "Secret things should be kept secret." Prov. 11:13. To get there through the heart one has to learn to control its wanderings. This is what the scripture in 2 Cor. 10 terms taking captive the thoughts of the heart. These are wrong thoughts, lies, which Satan projects in order to challenge the word of truth in the heart of man. They act as strongholds and give rise to sinful acts. They can develop habitually, and have to be ejected through prayers, the Word and right thinking. Our thoughts should centre on how to grow in grace through righteousness. The battle of the mind, which is considered the most difficult, takes quite some time to achieve and to maintain. We are all striving. Phil. 4:13 reads, "I can do all things through Christ Which strengthnest me." God created our hearts, which is supposed to be the abode of the Holy Spirit for His own purpose. It is man's responsibility to keep the heart clean through the power of the Holy Spirit. Heb. 8:10 reads, "For this is the covenant that I will make with the house of Israel after those days says the Lord. I will put My laws in their minds, and write them in their hearts; and I will be their God, and they shall be My people."

David was referred to as a man after God's own heart. Although he contended with a lot of challenges, he maintained a heart totally devoted to the love of God. On those few occasions that he sinned, he repented immediately, and never went back to those sins again. King

David understood better than most that God judges the heart of a man. Before his death he made a large personal offering of $100 million dollars for the construction of the house of God. He offered with his entire heart and out of love. He did not do this because he expected any further blessing from God nor because he was soliciting the praises of man. This is a habit which God wants us to develop in giving. It is Christlike. As he gave, he prayed in 1 Chr. 29:17-18, saying, "I know also my God, that Thou triest the heart, and hast pleasure in uprightness. As for me in the uprightness of my heart I have willingly offered these things, and now have I seen with joy thy people, which are present here to offer willingly unto Thee." He gave according to his heart, not expecting anything. This is like the way God gives by grace, not like man, who gives by circumstance. Any gift given unsacrificially, and without love may be perceived as worthless. 1 Cor. 13:3.

The Evangelical Christian

All Christians are supposed to be preaching the gospel of the Kingdom in one way or the other to unbelievers as an act of obedience to the general call in Matt. 28:18-20, which reads, "All power is given unto Me in heaven and in earth. Go ye therefore and make disciples of all the nations, baptising them in the Name of the Father, and of the Son, and of the Holy Spirit. Teaching them to observe all things whatsoever I have commanded you; And lo, I am with you always even unto the end of the world." There are also echoes of this call in Jon. 20-21; Lk. 24:47-49; Mk. 16:15-16; Acts 1:8. This is also a move towards Christlikeness.

Some Reasons Why Christians Should Lead People to Christ

All Christians are supposed to reproduce themselves spiritually. There should be a period of follow-up after evangelism until the convert attains spiritual growth. I must confess that I am not good at this follow ups. Follow-ups can involve visitations and are more effective and better when done in groups of two or three, not singly. It requires a lot of patience and communication. The commission to win souls runs contrary to the agenda of the evil one. He wants to keep humans continually ignorant of the Truth of the Word of God. In Hos. 4:6 God Himself said: "My people are destroyed because of lack of knowledge; because thou hast rejected knowledge I will also reject thee, that thou shalt be no priests to me; seeing thou hast forgotten the law of thy God, I will also forget thy children." It is the teaching of the Holy Spirit through the Word that imparts Christlikeness. A believer who does not read and study the Word will neither attain a Christlike nature nor be able to make others do so. Jam. 4:17 states that failing to do that which you are supposed to do is a sin. This means that failing to read and sturdy the word and to evangelise is a sin.

The Spirit behind salvation is the spirit of forgiveness and love. This is the message of evangelism. Love does not end in communication, but in demonstration. About twenty years ago I felt that it would be more comfortable for me to pray for people very seriously inside my room to give their lives to Christ. I had compiled a long list, which I put in a file. As I was kneeling down in my bedroom, earnestly asking God to touch each soul, a voice spoke to me immediately and said: "Go to the streets and talk to them there." A more serious call also came later. Mk. 16:1.

In evangelism one is supposed to minister with love, patience and human concern, which is the way Christ taught us. The fact that Christ was all the while waiting patiently for us sinners to come back to Him while still supplying our needs should teach us to be patiently disposed towards those we evangelise on. Always pray that God will keep new converts protected against satanic deception and manipulations in Jesus's Name.

Chapter Four

— BY PRAYERS —

"But if from thence thou shalt seek the Lord thy God, thou shalt find Him, if thou seek Him with all thy heart and with all thy soul."

Deut.4:29

We shall remain strangers to God our Creator if we do not pray consistently. Some of our prayers lack fervency. There is no sincerity, persistence and fire in the manner and substance of some of our prayers. Sometimes the requests are not in agreement with the Word of God. Some spiritual problems require a steady, persistent, aggressive conflict through prayers. The scriptures said in Is. 66:9: "'Shall I bring to birth and not cause to bring forth?' saith the Lord. 'Shall I cause to bring forth and shut the womb? Shall I deliver without labour?'" Is. 66:8 reads: "For as soon as Zion was in labour, she gave birth to her child." This is a confirmation that travail in the spirit during prayers facilitates answers. We have all experienced unanswered prayers several times over. Luke 22:44 describes the way Jesus travailed in prayers at Gethsemane. "And being in an agony He prayed more earnestly: and His sweat was as it were great drops of blood falling down to the ground." God strengthened him after the prayers for His Own divine Will on earth. Even Jesus experienced unanswered prayers. David tore his clothes and put on rags and ashes on his body on specific occasions he prayed to God; and so did Hezekiah and others.

The first priority of the early Christian Church was faithfulness in prayers. The spiritual warfare of that time needed to be addressed. When Jesus lived in this world the least window of opportunity he had He hastened to a quiet place in order to pray and commune with His beloved Heavenly Father. In the book of Luke 22:46, He said to His disciples: "Why sleep ye? Rise and pray lest ye enter into temptation." This is the same message that He is giving us today. Do we pray often enough and rightly? All believers are required to pray unceasingly, whether they are happy or unhappy, prepared for prayers or not, tired or strengthened, convenient or not. Continuity leads to success.

In Ps. 2:8 God said to Jesus: "Ask of Me and I will give Thee the heathen for Thine inheritance. And the uttermost part of the earth for Thine possession." He did not because He was His beloved Son exempt Him from praying for His requests. This shows that Jesus also had to follow the due process of praying to God.

The message is clear. If you do not ask, you will not receive. You will receive that which you ask for in prayers provided you do so according to the will of God. Sometimes people are too tired to pray seriously in the night. This attitude will not get anyone anywhere and opens doorways for the enemy to enter and reinforce that habit. 1 Cor. 5:6 reads: "...a little leaven leavens the whole lump."

Jesus is the Great High Priest that is always waiting to receive our prayers. Heb. 4:14 reads: "Seeing then that we have a great High Priest that is passed into the heavens, Jesus the Son of God, let us hold fast our profession for we have not a High Priest which cannot be touched with the feeling of our infirmities; but was in all points tempted like as we are, yet without sin. Let us therefore come boldly unto the throne of grace that we may obtain mercy and find grace to help in time of need." Grace walks on righteousness and requires a lot of prayers. Christ is disappointed with those who give up easily in prayers instead of continuing. This is unfortunate because He has already won the victory at the Cross. It may be that a little further perseverance in prayers is needed to receive the answer.

I once had a problem which God made me believe would take a long time to sort out. Friends, out of sympathy, suggested many short-term solutions that would negate the Word of God. I thank God that I found the grace to reject all the negative advice. I persisted fervently in prayers and claimed the victory 14 years after. God is never too late. Is. 62:6b-7 reads: "Ye that make mention of the Lord, do not keep silent, and give Him no rest till He establishes. And till he makes Jerusalem a praise in the earth." If we pray aright and live righteously, our journey there will be easier. It is the intention of the evil one to keep Christians from communicating with God in prayers.

How Do We Pray Aright?

1. Pray in an honest and sincere manner. Pro. 28:9
2. Pray with faith. Heb. 11:6
3. Pray with love and a forgiving spirit. Math. 6:12
4. Pray in the Name of Jesus. Jon. 14:13-14
5. Pray in holiness. 1 Jon. 3:22
6. Pray according to the Will of God. 1 Jon. 5:14

7. Pray quoting the Word of God. Jon. 15:7
8. Pray fervently. Jam. 5:14
9. Pray in the spirit. Eph. 6:18
10. Pray unceasingly. 1 Thess. 5:17
11. Pray with humility. 2 Chr. 7:14
12. Pray patiently, consistently and intensively. Dan. 10:2-3
11. Pray for others, including your enemies. Matt. 5:44
12. Pray agreement prayers. Matt. 18:19
13. Pray with reverence and love. Matt. 6:9-10
14. Pray in the Name of Jesus, according to His Nature and character. Jon. 14:13, 15

We are aware that prayer is a two-way communication between God and man. It is where issues are clarified, and solutions to problems arrived at. The feedback may take any of these forms.

1. It will be granted.
2. Hold on (timing is wrong).
3. Go and amend your ways first.
4. No, not right or proper for you.
5. No (silence due to sin).
6. Process already in action.
7. Unclear request/incorrect approach.

Some people specialise in writing letters of their requests to God. It is also good; but know that God Himself has His own requests for you too which may look like this. "Child try and secure salvation first. Give up your selfish ways and show love to others. Live a humble life because I give grace to the humble and My grace threads on righteousness. Have faith in my ability to solve your problems. Obey my Word and spread the gospel to others. As you do these things you will notice that the answers to your requests will begin to be released."

The Lord once said to me, "I can only cover in obedience." Rom. 5:19. Before we begin to table further requests to God, let us ask ourselves how many of His we have taken care of. He is as desperate for us to answer His requests as we are that ours should meet His approval. It is not the length of prayers that matters but the truthfulness and fervency. Righteousness, faith, a forgiving heart and humility are necessary in order to have prayers answered.

In Luke. 16:20-23 Lazarus the beggar might have been praying and expecting the healing of his wounds, but it did not happen because things have to go according to the will of God. While the dogs were still licking his wounds, God was busy getting his mansion in Heaven ready while Father Abraham was expecting him.

When God promised Abraham a son, nothing happened after ten years. Then He returned the second time and spoke to him and said: "Walk before Me and be blameless." Gen. 17:1. He continued in faith and prayers, and claimed a son as a result of his obedience. Paul's prayer in 2 Cor. 12:8 was not answered the way he expected, but he surrendered to God.

A righteous man may have his prayers always answered; but as soon as he falls into sin and fails to repent and plead for forgiveness, his prayers may cease to be answered. If he also refuses to forgive others, he may not have his sins forgiven and prayers answered. The act of nurturing negative thoughts is as a result of bitterness and unforgiveness. All sins are against God and the punishment for them will eventually come from Him. It may not be easy for some of us, but our prayers need to reflect more genuine love than accusations. The spirit of prayer is that of love. This demands extreme carefulness with unrepentant deadly enemies. One has a right to pray and call for the protection of God. The power of life and death are God's.

In the outline of the Lord's Prayer, which Jesus gave His disciples for all, there are seven patterns of requests. Matt. 6:9-13. There may be a need to reproduce all of them as the need arises. It is the Holy Spirit that energises our prayers. Prayer is often regarded as the most vital part of the believer's life. It is where the pressure on the life of the believer can be eased. It is our nearest link to Jesus and to God. Some may wonder why according to 1 Thess. 5:17 we have to pray unceasingly. These are some of the reasons.

1. Prayer activates one's faith. Jam. 5:15
2. It establishes a closer connection between man and God. Is. 1:18
3. It is the only way to defeat our enemies. Num. 16:29
4. A possible way of averting the wrath and judgement of God. Ez. 22:30
5. Healing and deliverance come by praying. Jam. 5:14-15
6. It brings the forgiveness of sins without which salvation will not work. 1 Jon. 1:8-9
7. It is the path of holiness. Luke. 22:46
8. It is a way to sound the opinion of God about oneself. Matt. 7:7
9. Repentance comes through prayers.
10. Prayers put Satan off. Ps. 91:15

Satan can come in to disrupt things in a life by claiming that that person did not pray to God or read the Word that day, and as a result has let the door open for him to enter. Answers to prayers do not always have to be instant as has been discussed earlier. The ten lepers whom Jesus healed and asked to go and show themselves to the priest only received their healing while they were on their way. Lk.17:12.

Many people in the Old Testament received instant answers when they prayed.

Moses. Ex. 32:11-14.

Elijah. 1 Kin. 18:36-38.

Abraham. Gen. 20-17.

The Disciples of Christ. Lk. 10-17.

Hezekiah. 2 Kin. 19:15-20.

Esther. Est. 4:16, 5:1-5.

Gideon. Gid. 6:39-40.

Jacob. Gen. 32:9-12, 24-30.

Many Christians feel that their prayers are answered because their needs continue to be met in one way or the other. They are also hopeful of outstanding breakthrough from God. God is very patient and merciful those years that He is waiting for us to repent. He can continue to meet our daily needs to make us come to an understanding of how merciful and good He is. He can use both blessings and punishment to bring about a turnaround in the lives of people. The Word of God states that because the punishment for sin is not executed immediately, the man of sin tends to continue in sin. Ecc. 8:11. As far as God is concerned, as sinners our prayers are an abomination to Him. Prov. 28:9. They will cease to be so only when we repent and give them up.

I was interceding for the life of a believer who became a born again Christian before me and is a pastor in a Church. His answer came immediately to the effect that I should pray rather for the salvation of her soul. I was shocked to discover that this same person needed prayers for salvation. The relevant point here is that God, Who searches the heart of man, is the only one Who can understand and reveal the hidden things in man. He knows us better than we know ourselves. Dan. 2:22 reads: "He reveals deep and secret things. He knows what is in the darkness. And light dwells with Him."

Chapter Five

— BY RIGHTEOUSNESS —

"For He made Him Who knew no sin to be sin for us, that we might become the righteousness of God in Him." 2 Cor.5:21

Righteousness is not man's achievement, but a gift of grace given to man by God through Jesus. God preached righteousness to Abraham in Gen. 1:17 and he obeyed and attained grace. The law was waiting for Jesus Christ to come to establish faith in the righteousness of God, so that man can obey it. It can be said that the birth of Christ was the birth of the righteousness of God. Only Jesus can baptise with the Holy Spirit, Who can make that righteousness possible in the heart of man. He is also that Narrow way. In Lk. 13:24 Jesus said, "Strive to enter in at the straight gate, for many I say unto you will seek to enter in and shall not be able." This is because repentance and faith are required.

Faith is the obedience to the instructions of God, and this results in righteousness.

It is the reluctance to repent that brings condemnation to man in the end. Genuine repentance is followed by the remission of sin. This is why Jesus said in Matt. 21:31 that harlots, thieves and tax collectors who truly repented will enter the Kingdom, but that those people expected to enter would not because they lacked repentance and faith. Flesh and blood cannot inherit the kingdom. It has to be transformed into the righteousness of the Son of God.

The work of faith responds positively to the will of God. When we obey God, we are living out our faith. As believers the blood of Jesus has cleansed our conscience from dead works so that we can devote our thoughts and ways towards the service of God. Faith and righteousness are to our salvation as blood and water are to human life.

In the parable of the wedding feast the man who in isolation was not wearing the garment for the wedding feast was immediately sent away. Matt. 22:11. He was not clothed in faithfulness, righteousness and obedience. Faith activates obedience. It activates the power of God in our lives, because Christ is convinced that we are serious. It is also indicative of man's love for God. Once the power of the Holy Spirit moves in a life, the evil one will try to attack or bring delay. Once you receive an instruction from God he will try to suggest a way to disobey it sooner or later. Once he recognises the way you receive from God, he will try to masquerade it so that you will think that it is God talking to you. God has given us a firm assurance in the book of Is. 54:15 which reads: "Behold they shall surely gather together but not by Me. Whosoever shall gather together against thee, shall fall for thy sake." We need to pray that the Holy spirit will search our hearts for sin as often as possible, and be ready to accept His conviction, correction and change. This merciful gesture of the Holy Spirit should lead us into a continuous habit of repentance and sanctification.

Sin is often referred to as wickedness. The scripture in Isa. 48:22, which reads, "There is no peace says my God for the wicked," establishes the need for a daily confession of sins. The punishment for sin has been established since the creation of the world. It requires blood for cleansing. In the old covenant, Moses had to sprinkle the tabernacle with blood; and the blood of animals was shed to cleanse human sins. This act of purification did not really penetrate the heart. God was all this while preparing for the real and innocent blood of Christ for a perfect cleansing of the soul. This will provide that righteousness which the law demands. Two relevant points that should not be underestimated:

1. The whole length of time, even centuries, and effort it took God to put together and perfect the way of salvation for man.
2. What agony Christ went through on this earth in order to shed the precious blood that would wash away the sins of those who would believe. He had to endure the fact that his righteous body had to receive all our sins and iniquities willingly; the despicable way in which He was tortured; the thirty-nine stripes; the excruciating pain, shame, disgrace and agony that He was made to pass through. Based on all these, the need for humans to give salvation the seriousness it deserves can never be overestimated. I have always asked this question: Can God, Who allowed His beloved son to pass through such an excruciating pain because of man's sin, now spare the same sin that gave rise to all this pain and suffering? Even to the rational mind it does not sound right. Ps. 94:10 reads: "He that chastiseth the heathen, will He not correct?" These facts establish that salvation is the ultimate reality in the life of any human. It is the life and death issue that we need to sort out before any other matter on this earth. Matt. 6:33.

As believers we need to accept the merciful conviction of the Holy Spirit that is supposed to lead to genuine repentance and the remission of sins. There is a question that needs to be asked every time.

What are We Doing in the Territory of the Devil?

The territory of the devil is that of sin and its consequences. It has one pathway to its destination: sin to death and death to Hell. Jesus said to the Pharisee in Jon. 8:24, "Therefore I say to you that you will die in your sins; for if you do not believe that I am He, you will die in your sins." These words were spoken with a deep feeling of love and seriousness. Unfortunately, the meaning was not grasped.

Sin is Satan's passion and badge. If we spend our entire life trying to get rid of it, and eventually succeed, to God be all the glory; we have achieved the purpose for which we came into the world. Christ is the Word. Jon. 1:1 says, "In the beginning was the Word, and the Word was with God, and the Word was God." To get out of the territory of Satan you have to step out of it first by submitting to God through obedience to the Word. If you resist Satan by obeying the Word, he will flee. If you know the Word you will implement Jesus' Words in Jon. 3:5 which states, "Except a man be born again of water and of the Spirit, he will not enter the kingdom of heaven". Jam. 4:17 reads, "Therefore to him who knows to do good and does not do it, to him it is sin. This is also referred to as the sin of omission. Every sin, immediately positions one directly in the territory of Satan, and establishes the need to get out as soon as possible. If, for example, you are supposed to help the less privileged while in a position to do so, and you do not, it is a sin of omission because the Word of God says: "Bear ye each other's burdens and fulfil the laws of Christ. Gal. 6:2. Knowing the Word of God and compromising it in order to make life easier for one is indirectly stepping into the territory of the devil. Sin immediately opens a doorway of entry for the evil one to attack. If a believer continues in sin, although the person is claiming to be born again and quoting the Word of God, the devil himself will be making claims on the person's life. Rom. 6:16 reads, "Do you not know that to whom you present yourself slaves to obey, you are that one's slave whom you obey, whether of sin leading to death, or of obedience leading to righteousness?" The only way out of sin is through the grace of Christ, and faith is the motivator. When attacks would seem overwhelming, let your confidence and faithfulness in Christ's victory be a source of encouragement to you. Ps. 94:19.

It would seem as if Satan is indirectly warning believers to make sure that they do not stray into his territory. If mistakenly they trespass into this territory, he will welcome this as a challenge. He rules it very jealously with his rulers and demons, and carefully scrutinises the narrow line of demarcation between righteousness and sinfulness. If our lives are in agreement with that of Jesus, the evil one will not find it easy to steal, kill or destroy in our territory.

There were no Laws of Moses or the Ten Commandments in the days of Abraham; he just followed God in faith and obedience. This is the way that God wants us to follow Christ, without relying on our strength or works and in obedience to the Holy Spirit.

Sin destroys the spiritual life of man. We need salvation to restore it. God will be reluctant to operate in an atmosphere of sin in the life of believers. He will rather have that sin repented of and remitted. He may decide to use that interval to teach some relevant lessons. Many step into the territory of Satan either through weakness or ignorance. If God in His mercy gives a chance to repent, and that chance is not taken, that person's salvation may eventually be lost. Heb. 10:26-27. This is because God will not allow anybody to bring the property of Satan into His Kingdom. He does not want all those sins listed in Gal. 5:19-21, which reads, "Now the works of the flesh are evident, which are adultery, fornication, uncleanness, lewdness, idolatry, sorcery, hatred, contentions, jealousies, outbursts of wrath, selfish ambitions, dissensions, heresies, envy, murders, drunkenness, revelries, and the like; of which I tell you beforehand just as I always told you in times past, that those who practice such things will not inherit the Kingdom of God."

The scripture states that God will have mercy on those who fear Him from one generation to the other. Fear motivates obedience. When you fear God, you will always strive to see how to obey Him. When you fear man, your greatest wish will be to please that person; if it is the world standard you fear that you may not attain, you will be striving to achieve that standard.

There is no punishment in this world that can be compared to life in Hell. This is what Christ came to save us from. He destroyed that life of Hell at the Cross for those who would repent and believe. and is asking us to accept the eternal life He received from God. Hos. 13:14 reads, "I will ransom them from the power of the grave. I will redeem them from death. O death I will be your plagues. O grave I will be your destruction." The territory of the devil positions men in hell. Man's greatest fear is of death. Christ is asking man to accept the free gift of eternal life which God made possible through him and most are hesitant. How can one refuse life and accept death in hell?

The Word in Eph. 5:27 was specific and stated that Christ would come to rapture a glorious Church without spot or wrinkles. This is the standard of God's righteousness. While we are still around today, breathing His air and enjoying the universe He created, let us make sure that we are saved and our lives secured in Christ. Let us always strive to be detached from the territory of the evil one, and live every day in preparation as if it is our last.

Those who have not given their lives to Christ according to Jon. 3:5, are advised to do so, and become members of Christ's Spiritual Body, the Church. All believers who have received the gift of the Holy Spirit are united in one spirit with each other and with Christ. If you are not born again, any mistakes made through ignorance unbelief or insufficient knowledge of the Word may prove destructive in the end. You can even condemn yourself ignorantly by your own words in the same way that I once did before I was born again. The answer immediately came to me. It said, "You have just condemned yourself." Jam. 1:26. You can even be attributing the glory of God to yourself or to another and can even have blood on your hands without knowing it. This is because there is no indwelling of the Holy Spirit to guide you on the path of righteousness. A divine voice that spoke to me said: "If it is sin, run for your life." Ezek. 18 4b. We are supposed to grow into the image of the Son of God, but many have grown into the likeness of the image of the evil one and he is claiming to identify with them because of this.

Chapter Six

— THE HOLD OF THE WORD —

"The Words that I speak to you are spirit, and they are life. "Jon. 6:63

The Word of God is the Word of truth. Jn. 8:32. Jesus is the Truth. Jon. 14:6. The Holy Spirit is the Spirit of truth. He operates in the minds of believers in order to effect a change through the Word. The Three work closely together. With God the Father, they are all joined in the same purpose, plan and power. We are to walk in the truth of the Word of God, because it will live in us forever, and not allow the ways of the world to distract our mind. We are given the Word to guide us away from sin in the world. When we have a good knowledge and understanding of the Word, we can make right decisions, and relate kindly with people in the world. The decisions we make can either justify or condemn us, in view of the fact that in the world we have tribulations, Jon. 16:33. In the family there may be foundational problems, 1 Cor. 3:11, and that we can operate in the midst of adverse circumstances. We are therefore required to be carefully guided by the Word if we expect to eventually avoid the condemnation of God's judgement in the end. It is understood that we are all born in sin, Ps. 51:5, but the Word of God is given to guide us away from sin through the empowerment of the Holy Spirit. Zech. 4:6.

When we allow the Word to be embodied in us, we can be transformed into the likeness of Christ. It provides all the necessary materials required to understand Our Creator and also man's obligations to Him. The Word provides a solution to all the problems of life and reveals the promises of God for those who would believe. Some, when problem arises, ignore the scripture and impatiently rush to the world for a solution. As a result of this impulsive decision, doorways are opened for more sin.

In Jon. 6:63 Jesus said, "These words are life, they are spirit." This means that if they are thoughtfully and truthfully read and meditated on, they can be activated into life by the Holy Spirit dwelling in the lives of believers. Jon. 8:51 states, "Verily, verily I say unto you, if a man keeps my saying he shall never see death." This is the second death. The Word can be regarded as the pillar on which our Christian faith rests. It is the guiding light of our journey to

Heaven. The continuous reading, meditation and practice of the Word restores the spiritual life of man which died at the fall. Without a serious study and meditation, the Word can only pass through a person and depart. It will not enter the mind to remain. Jon.15:7. The book of Jon. 1:1 presents the Word in its divine form and nature. This is the Living Word, the Son of God through Whom He spoke all existence into being. The Word is also referred to as the Living Water Which one drinks and will never thirst again. It will fill the person with a natural overflow of the fullness of the Spirit of God. Jon. 4:10-14. It is through the Word that you can develop the attributes of God, which is also that of Christ's.

Disobedience to the Word creates a serious doorway through which the enemy immediately enters in order to operate. This is why it is necessary to understand the Word properly and to obey it at all costs. A divine voice said to me, "Even if you have to die doing it." Matt. 10:22b. The enemy operates in every area of disobedience whether the person is a believer or not. Everybody needs to be continuously washed and cleansed by the Living Water, which is the Word of God. This will get rid of the daily contaminations we pick up in our minds in our daily interactions with people who share contrary and hostile views of the scripture, defiled places we visited, and the distractions of the world, etc. Both the mind and thoughts need to be soaked again in the Word in order to reunite with Christ spiritually. Jesus said to His disciples, "You are already clean because of the Word that I spoke to you." Jon. 15:3. It is necessary that on reading the Word it should be allowed to remain so that it will work its transformation in the mind. Rom. 10:17 reads, "So then faith comes by hearing, and hearing by the Word of God."

Faith is a response to the Word in a trusting, childlike manner. The lack of understanding of the Word of God can be said to be a reason why faith is weak, and some believe that Christianity is too much of a struggle. This is because the Word has not been given enough time and thought. The heart was not made fertile for it to grow.

Lack of knowledge of the Word of God can lead to spiritual disaster. Just as the devil cannot masquerade the blood of Jesus, he also cannot change the Word of God, which is eternal and immutable.

Chapter Seven

— THE DIVINE LOVE —

"And above all things have fervent love for one another, for love will cover a multitude of sins." 1 Pet. 4:8

In the book of Mk. 12:29-31 Jesus, in reply to a question on which commandment was the first replied, "The first of all Commandments is, Hear O Israel The Lord our God The Lord is one. And you shall love the Lord your God with all your heart, with all your soul, with all your mind, and with all your strength. This is the first commandment. And the second like it is this: You shall love your neighbour as yourself. There is no other commandment greater than these." God is Love, and lack of love is responsible for all the problems of mankind. In Him dwells the fullness of love. All the true love in the world comes from Him. When the love of God dwells in you then you will be able to relate it to others, and to love others as you do yourself.

In this new dispensation a new standard and motive for love is set. It reads in Jon. 15:12, "A new Commandment I give unto you, that ye love one another; as I have loved you. That ye also love one another." We know that Christ's love for man is total, sacrificial and true. He loved to death. He wants us to love exactly the way He did. It is the Holy Spirit indwelling believers Who puts the understanding of God and His love inside man's minds. This love motivates obedience.

This Christian (divine) love is sacrificial and responds to insults and injustices not with retaliation but with tolerance, and forgiveness and prayers. Prayers are to ease off the pain of being hurt. Christ's sensitivity and divine compassion towards human weaknesses, pain and suffering clearly mirrors His selfless sacrificial love. The love of God which is that of Christ goes far beyond the personal to others. Jesus was the Love of God that came to live in a world without love.

The love that is centred on kind relationships with others, wars against selfishness, instils the fear of God, and makes believers obey the Word of God.

The good Samaritan in Lk. 10:30-37 was a good example of one who extended genuine love to the neighbour he did not know. Under normal circumstances that man would turn his back on the good Samaritan for he himself belonged to the clan rejected by society.

Jesus was born in very humble circumstances and His ministry and life assumed the same pattern. This is the will of God; for according to 1 Cor. 13:4, "love vaunteth not itself, is not puffed up." He did not come to the world in His divine form, majesty, glory, honour and wealth, etc. He needed to teach a serious lesson of growing in divine love, humility and faith which would change the destiny of man. This love is termed the way of perfection, because God Himself Who is love is perfect and Christ is the embodiment of this love. It is the most important virtue to develop, without which one is headed towards Hell. It goes hand in hand with sacrificial service and humility. It is the primary fruit of the Spirit. Jesus summarised the whole essence of love in Jon. 14:15 by saying, "If ye love me keep my commandments." If you sing loving songs and praises to God every day, and help those in need, but without love, He may not exactly understand the love you are making reference to. He wants to see love in everything you do. Obedience to God is indicative of love for Him.

The scripture in 1 Cor. 13 on divine love is self-explanatory. It shows love as priceless. Any time spent in developing this virtue is time very well spent. The human consciousness of love should be practiced twenty-four hours every day. If our actions are motivated by divine love every day, we may be able to live through the commandments without the usual difficulties.

When we give because we have figured out that giving is necessary, we may have done well, but did we give with love? Did we have compassion for the pain and suffering of the person and give out of a desperate need to lessen the discomfort? If not, our gifts may not produce the fruits we expect. If we give in anger or competitively, our gifts may not be acceptable before God, for He loves a cheerful giver; and anger is not from the Holy Spirit. If one operates in the gift of the spirit without love and humility, then the person is not glorifying God or edifying the Church. If a life is puffed up and without love, it is worth nothing and spiritually useless to God. If one lives a selfish life and causes offence to others, the person has no love. Love, like grace, thrives on everlasting righteousness and is faithful to the end. Pro. 10:12b states, "Love covereth all sins." The act of getting there is walking in the love of God in all things, all the days of our lives. The divine instruction given to me recently emphasised 'everlasting righteousness,' Dan. 9:24, which is everlasting love.

Agape love extends to people of different races, colours, nationalities and religious inclinations. You may not approve of some people, but based on the wisdom of God, you still have to show love to them. When Jesus started His Ministry, He was misunderstood, as a national leader of one group of people. He explained that His Kingdom was international, not restrictive to one. He came to extend the love of God to repentant sinners also. In Jon. 10:16 He said, "And other sheep I have which are not of this fold; them also I must bring and; they will hear My Voice; and there will be one flock and one Shepherd."

Jesus said that we should love our enemies and pray for them. Prayer is an act of love. They need sympathy and prayers because some may have gone beyond the understanding of the consequences of their actions. This does not mean that one has to condone their sins.

It is this divine love that made God create us in His own image and likeness. Can you imagine how privileged we are to be considered worthy of this? He could have made us round, triangular, oblong and crawling on the ground in order to match our oncoming wickedness, if He so desired. But being that He is perfected in love, He gave us His goodness. It was also His love that made Him put man originally in the garden of Eden, to take part in the rulership of His creation. It is also the reason why He did not wipe the whole world out but spent thousands and thousands of ages planning a way to rescue man from the fall, by allowing the innocent blood of His beloved Son to be shed for our ransom.

One writer pointed out the fact that the closest we can get to the love of God, which is still beyond our imagination, is to just love our neighbours as ourselves. A song writer wrote about the love we cannot know until we depart from this world. Originally God planned to relate to us as father to a child. Unfortunately, our disobedience made it that of a king and rebellious subject. Today, the victory for the change has been won at the Cross and everything that is happening today is under the jurisdiction of God, Who is taking over the direct rulership of the earth again and restoring back all that the enemy has stolen. Man is currently witnessing the unfolding of God's plan for restoration, including all the elements he created. They are also crying out for restoration to their original condition. Rom. 8:21 reads, "...because the creation itself also will be delivered from the bondage of corruption into the glorious liberty of the children of God."

Because of His love for man, God has made His promises available to those who will believe in the sacrifice at the Cross. Through Christ's atonement God has made available the gifts of grace and faith that lead to eternal life, the Holy Spirit, His Word, the blood of Jesus, the power in the Name of Jesus and the power to pray and communicate with

Him. Everything that will make man's rescue and salvation possible has been released to those who believe and are willing. This is a perfect show of unconditional love. To perfect this love Jesus hung in total surrender at the Cross. My dear brethren, what more can we expect, seeing that He has emptied Himself for us?

God's chastisements are administered for the interest of love, and His punishments are remedial and for repentance. He forgives when the individual repents.

We demonstrate our love for our neighbours by bearing each other's burden, not doing to others what we would not like to be done to us, having compassion for people's pain and problems, forgiving one another, interceding for others, not causing offence, not judging or slandering or departing from the Ten Commandments. If you truly love your neighbour, you will not want to bring the ills of the Ten Commandments against them.

Love is not how you lead but how you serve others. According to the scripture in Matt. 5:43-47 one is supposed to love their enemies. Initially any attempt to do this may produce a feeling of unease. It is advisable to start by sympathising and interceding for them so that the anger will begin to go. It is only through love that one can be able to forgive serious sins. Prayers are needed for this.

Love is a uniting factor in the body of Christ. A Church that lacks love lacks unity. Discrimination and self-seeking will be common. It is the Holy Spirit Who puts the Love of God in the mind of man. This is why salvation is being born again of water and the Spirit.

A marriage that is based on God's divine love will be able to battle against all physical and spiritual oppositions. A married person that compromises the Word of God in order to maintain peace in the family can be said to have no love for God. Sin should be addressed and not condoned, and prayers rendered against it. An evangelist who lacks love can make salvation appear too difficult for new converts. Salvation is based on the love of God. Deliverance candidates are always frightened of deliverance ministers who minister without love. This can lead to fear instead of a greater feeling of faith. Jesus ministered and spoke the language of compassion. He put aside His glory in Heaven and came in the form of man to die the death of a criminal, because of love for God His Father and for man. The Holy Spirit has been in the world since the day of Pentecost, carrying the burden of lost souls, and labouring tirelessly to get people converted and saved. This is the love of God for man. David could not hurt Saul because of love, despite the fact that Saul desperately sought to kill him. 1 Sam. 18:5-22. John the Baptist lived in the wilderness clothed in camel's hair and ate only honey and locusts because he bore the burden of love for the lost souls. Matt. 3:1-4. Daniel fasted and interceded for twenty-one days for the forgiveness and restoration of Israel. As one intercedes for those who hurt them, a feeling of sympathy may replace that of hurt, leading to forgiveness.

It would appear as if the arrival of Jesus in humble and poor circumstances did not meet with the expectation of a huge giant descending in pomp and splendour to deliver the people from the Romans. It would have been unfortunate because that type of appearance might have given the wrong impression of what salvation is all about to man. Jesus lived exactly what He taught. He was faithful, loving, meek and humble, obedient to death, enduring and forgiving, gentle, kind and merciful, patient and self-controlled. He came to set an example of how to get there in a loveless world of sin, deceit, pain and vanity.

God's Love for Mankind

The journey to the Kingdom is encouraged by an appreciation of the love of God for mankind. However, the deep nature of this love cannot be fully understood by man on this earth. We can only catch a breath of it here and there. The scripture in Jon. 3:16 sums it up by saying, "For God so loved the world, that He gave His only begotten

Son, that whosoever believeth in Him, should not perish but have everlasting life." If He loved less, He would not have given the best He had. How are we receiving that best today? God Himself witnessed the excruciating pain, torture, agony, humiliation and derision that His beloved innocent Son Jesus was made to pass through because of love. Do you wonder that He said to Him, "Sit at My right hand; till I make Your enemies Your footstool."

Although those whom God referred to as His special people hurt Him so much because they rejected His gift of Love in Jesus, His punishment towards them was always remedial so that they could come back to Him. Isa. 26:9b reads, "For when your judgements are on the earth the inhabitants of the world will learn righteousness." He always cherished the day when the repentant remnants would return to Him so that He would bless them and wipe away their tears. Jesus said in Rev. 3:19, "As many as I love I rebuke and chasten." God desires nothing but peace and love between Himself and mankind. In Matt. 23:37b, Jesus cried out against the sinful nature of the people and said, "How often would I have gathered thy children together, even as a hen gathereth her chickens under her wings, and ye would not."

Zeph. 3:17 reveals the depth of God's love for His people in the way He would rejoice, because they had forsaken their sins. God was always ready to demonstrate His deepest felt love for His people, if only they would walk according to His Will.

There is a problem with our human tendency to expect God to overlook some aspects of our sins. Complete obedience satisfies God's standard of love. This is not by might but by the power of His Holy Spirit. The fulness of His love is available to any genuine repentant sinner. It is not us, but the sin in us that He dissociates His Holy nature from. This is because it contradicts His purity. The defence of His holiness glorifies Him.

Rom. 8:35 reads: "Who can separate us from the love of Christ? Shall tribulation or distress, or persecution or famine, or nakedness or peril or the sword?" We should not allow the flesh, the world and the evil one to separate us from the love of God. A divine voice once asked me: "Do you know that there are people who love me more than you do?" 1 Jon. 5:3. The meaning was clear. Your love is not enough! I immediately realised that I had to work more seriously on the exercise of my love towards Him and my fellow human beings.

Chapter Eight

KILLING PRIDE

"Verily I say unto you except ye be converted and become as little children ye shall not enter into the Kingdom of heaven. "Math. 18:3

Pride and unbrokenness are defective character traits, and the attributes of the evil one. If pride disappears completely from a life, that life will become broken. Pride creates major hindrances to getting there. This chapter will start by explaining what the scriptures say about pride. Salvation is by grace not by works so that the false pride in man will not attribute it to his effort. The necessary effort that gave rise to the victory had been perfected by Christ. One purpose of salvation is to deliver man from the spirit of pride which is an inheritance from the devil; to instil humility, and attribute of Christ. From that day that He was born of humble parents in a manger, to that day when He was received by clouds and taken back to heaven, He wore that garment of extreme humility, and lived every bit of it. From the following Scriptures below it is clear that anybody who is interested in making heaven, had better begin to dissociate themselves with anything associated with pride; avoid doing things for public esteem.

Lk. 14:11 reads, "For whoever exalteth himself shall be abased, and he that humbleth himself shall be exalted." This means that if your high position came as a result of pride or the evil one, you stand the chance of losing it or being humiliated.

1 Pet. 5:6 reads, "Humble yourselves therefore under the mighty Hand of God, so that He will exalt you in due time." God exalts the humble. He gives grace to them, but the proud He sees from a far distance. Jam. 4:6. Without grace nobody can make the kingdom.

When Jesus lived on this earth there was no likeness of anything proud around Him. He surrounded Himself with humble men. His disciples were ordinary men he met on the street or river, while they were fishing. Like His Father, He picks humble people, puts His nature inside them, and empowers them to do mighty works like Him. Matt. 14:12-14. In Matt. 11:29 Jesus said, "Take my yoke upon you and learn of Me, for I am meek and lowly in heart and you will find rest for your soul."

Humility guarantees peace from God. Jesus is the model of humility to be emulated. Ps. 138:6 reads, "Though the Lord be high, yet hath He respect for the lowly, but the proud He knoweth from afar off." God is ever ready to attend to the needs of the lowly in heart but distances Himself from the proud, because that pride is contrary to His nature.

Jer. 13:15-17 reads, "Hear ye and give ear. Be not proud. For the Lord has spoken. But if you will not hear it, my soul will weep in secret places for your pride; and my eye shall weep sore and run down with tears." If God, through His love for us, is driven to bitter tears because of our refusal to give up pride, we are already heading towards Hell.

Phil. 2:7 reads, "He made Himself of no reputation, taking the form of a bondservant and coming in the physical likeness of a man. Christ chose to give up His glorious and majestic divine nature. From this change he led a humble, servant-like life, which eventually led to the total surrender of His soul and body to the humiliation, excruciating pain, shame, agony and derision at the Cross. This was in order to perfect the assignment which God gave to Him; for like His Father He did everything in perfection. His mind was the mind of God. They shared the same mind, plan and purpose.

The scripture in Phil. 2:5 says, "Let this mind be in you

which was also in Christ Jesus." The Love we have for God, which brings His close presence in our lives, results in humility and service to others. Humility overlooks transgression and does not give offence to any. It esteems others better than self. Meekness is a practical expression of humility.

Pride has to depart in order to allow humility to come in and replace it. Pride can be hidden and subtle. If you acquire self-respect through pride, you have to give it up and suffer the denial of self-respect in order to be restored to humility.

Almost about twenty-three years ago, as I went with members of my Church to the prayer city of the Church where prayers go on twenty-four hours a day (as of then I had been deeply hurt by many people), I saw something written in the sky directly opposite to where I was standing. Nobody else saw it. It read: "Pride and Unforgiveness, what is preventing you from making the Kingdom." I was very thoroughly shaken that night at midnight. I was determined to do something about it at all costs. Every time I thought that pride was gone I was reminded that it was still there. After about a year or two I began to cry out desperately to the Lord in prayers, to reveal to me the areas of pride that I had not addressed. He was merciful. He held two ends of a cream-coloured towel in his two hands, raised them up and said to me: "You must serve." I was reminded immediately of His washing of the disciples' feet and wiping them with a towel. It said it all. I began to rejoice because at least I had a clear picture of what to do. He has shown me His light in this situation of darkness. The Psalmist said in Ps. 27:2 that the Lord is his light and salvation. It is only through His light, which is the light of the gospel, that darkness and confusion can be dispelled. Arrogant and rebellious thoughts in the mind are strongholds that oppose the Word of God and need to be pulled down through the Word and strong warfare prayers.

Jesus touched a leper before healing him. Mk. 1:41 reads, "Then Jesus moved with compassion, stretched out His hands and touched him." It was not as if He could not command healing from a distance, but He was teaching a lesson of faith, humility and love at the same time. Only a few, if any, would like to touch a leper. We would rather pray from a distance.

In the book of John 14:12-13 Jesus said, "Verily, verily I say unto you, he that believeth in Me, the works that I do shall he do also; and greater works than these shall he do because I go to My Father. And whatsoever he shall ask in My Name that will I do, that the Father may be glorified in the Son." Taken literally the humility of Christ is apparent here in comparing His work to that of other human beings.

It is also an allusion to His short ministry. Believers who receive power will continue till the end of their lives. No one really can perform some of the miracles He did. He commanded the waves and the sea and they obeyed Him instantly. Matt. 8:24-27. He walked on the sea. Peter in trying to imitate Him almost drowned.

Most importantly He was able to do these things, because no sin was found in Him. There is no one who is sinless. God said that our righteousness is like a filthy rag. To compare His works with that of humans is a great show of humility.

Pride can be subtle and hidden. In my early days as a healing minister, we found ourselves praying for a pregnant woman about to deliver in the Church at a night vigil at 2 am. One of the nurses among us decided that she should be rushed to the hospital as fast as possible. At the hospital she made us to understand that she had to separate from the prospective husband when she discovered that he came from a clan that worshipped a snake as their god. My disappointment and distress over her situation was beginning to show in my face when I heard this and thought of the rush to get pregnant and the effect of the whole story on the unborn child who was conceived out of wedlock. We then decided to join hands and pray before leaving. As we prayed my spiritual eyes were opened to behold a figure clad in pure white standing before a wash basin with water held before him. A white piece of cloth was already over his mouth and nose. He was observing my impatient and worried reaction from His eyes which I thought were slightly turned towards me. Immediately I realised that I had done something very wrong. I was sent there to serve in love and humility not to be judgemental and impatient. The fact that a divine helper came to take delivery of that baby is an act of humility. God, who foresees the end from the beginning, already knows the length and breadth of that baby's journey on this earth. I repented and pleaded for forgiveness.

When Judas came with the unfortunate multitude to arrest Jesus, in Matt. 26:47-54, Peter immediately slashed off the ear of one of the high priest's servants. Jesus made him understand that the battle was not of that nature and had to be carried out according to the will of God. In His humility He bent down, picked up the ear and fixed it again. Lk. 22:51. He could easily have asked one of His disciples to pick it up and give to Him, but Jesus is humility.

When He informed His disciples in Matt. 16:21 of the type of suffering that would come His way, Peter strongly advised Him not to allow such a thing to be done to Him. Possibly, he thought that Jesus was too big to allow such a thing to happen in His life. It might also be that he out of love did not want anybody to hurt Jesus. Jesus in no uncertain terms made him understand that that was the way to the Kingdom. He knew that Satan had decided to bring Peter down, but Jesus had offered prayers to God for him.

If one cannot come to terms with suffering as a way of life in ministerial work, pride is responsible. If the mind is always set on self-defence instead of repenting and submitting to God, pride is responsible. Suffering, endurance and perseverance for Christ helps to develop the spirit of meekness and gentleness, which is part of the messianic ministry. It is advised that if the devil accuses you of any sin you know that you are guilty of, in the spirit of humility you should immediately repent and ask God for forgiveness. This will prevent the devil having to send a petition to God against you.

A child who is learning to walk often trips and falls. He looks up and laughs, expecting to be helped. He manages to pick himself up and repositions himself well for another attempt. The important fact here is that he takes the fall jovially, does not resent it or blame anybody. He sometimes blames himself by crying, but insists on continuing the effort until he succeeds. He persists in this until he perfects it and starts running. This is what humility, willingness, endurance and persistence is all about in the walk to the Kingdom. This is why Jesus said in Matt. 18:3, that except we become like little children we shall by no means enter the kingdom of heaven.

Ps. 94:18 reads, "If I say my foot slips, Your mercy O Lord will hold me up." One should not be ashamed of making mistakes. Whenever you fall in your walk to Heaven, get up, plead for forgiveness of sin, and continue after learning the appropriate lessons from the fall in order to be able to maintain consistency in the walk.

Ps. 94:19 reads, "In the multitude of my anxieties within me, Your comforts delight my soul." When you feel that the suffering is too much and begin to feel discouraged, the comforting presence of the Holy Spirit will quicken and refresh you.

When God blesses His children, in as much as they have to testify to this, He does not want them to show it off as if they earned it by merit. Humility demands that we give glory to God. Jesus endured the sins of man placed on His righteous body without complaint. The humility of Jesus is legendary. If we are fortunate enough to catch glimpses of it spiritually, we are bound to be thoroughly shaken and ashamed of ourselves for the rest of our lives. Humility cautions us not to do anything to attract attention to ourselves or to accept the praises that belong to God. Let everything be done to the glorify of God.

Chapter Nine
—SEPERATION UNTO GOD—

"Wherefore come out from among them and be ye separate, saith the Lord, and touch not the unclean thing and I will receive you." 2 Cor. 6:17

Separation is a theme that runs both through the Old and the New Testament in the Bible. Separation unto God generally is from sin to righteousness. The spirit of the world is not working according to the Spirit of God. The believer, although separated from the world, is still supposed to relate to people of the world in love. He is supposed to humbly serve the needs of the people and pray for both good and bad. He who is separated from the world ignores its transgressions and moves ahead because the world is the home of provocation and evil.

Separation can be described as a spiritual surgical means first devised and used by God to deliver His children from their evil foundation; to put apart the good from the evil;

to create access for Himself to reach out and minister to their needs; and to position them properly for Heaven. This method is still very much being used today. One can also be separated from the evil covenants and curses made by his or her ancestors. Those who were responsible for the death of Christ insisted that Jesus must die and that Barnabas, who rightly deserved death, should be released to them. They went ahead to declare that Christ's blood should be on them and their children. Matt. 27:25-26. By so doing they had brought a curse on their children. These are perfectly innocent children, heritage of God. Ps. 27:3. They were completely unaware of the change in their destinies. A need had been created for the children to be released and separated from that evil curse and covenants. That foundation needs deliverance.

In an evil foundation, you can repeatedly have any or some of these: idolatry, witchcraft, occultism, curses, evil covenants, polygamy, regular instances of premature death, abnormal immorality, lineage of poverty, accidents, marine lineage, barrenness, mental illness, unusual sudden deaths, divorce, regular instability, etc. Through prayers people can be delivered from all these.

Getting there may become a possibility after one has separated himself or herself from everything that the Word of God disapproves of by the help of the Holy Spirit.

Separation can be unto God, or from God. Hence it can be positive or negative. The scripture in 2 Tim. 3:1-7 and 1 Tim. 4:1-3 state that in these last days, many will forsake their faith for other gods and live contrary to what the Word teaches. This is a negative spiritual separation from God, and receiving the new birth is the positive one. Separation can be physical in the sense that you have decided to move away from the evil foundation of your origin. Separation can also be partial in the sense that after the separation one continues to experience some of the problems that led to the separation. When the separation is not spiritually complete, then there is a need to persevere in prayers and the Word, using all the weapons of warfare in Eph. 6:12-18.

The greatest act of separation is unto salvation, when Jesus used His blood to pay, once and for all, the price that would separate those who would believe in Him from the bondage of sin and death. Col. 2:14-15,

If you do not know Christ spiritually while you are on this earth, you will also not know Him when you leave this earth and get there. God is a spirit, and they that worship Him must worship Him in the spirit and in truth. Jon. 4:24. When you live according to the scriptures you are living in the spirit. Only the Holy Spirit can make this possible.

Salvation can be perceived to be either in two or three

stages. When you accept Jesus as Lord and Saviour and are baptised, that is the first stage. Your sins are forgiven. When you receive the gift of the Holy Spirit, He will begin to sanctify you, setting you apart for obedience; that is the second stage. When Jesus arrives for the rapture of the Church, salvation will be consummated. This is the final stage. Some merge the first and second stage together.

The Israelites were in Egypt for 400 years. For a greater part of those years they were in bondage, serving the Egyptians. Through miracles, signs and wonders God finally separated them from the Egyptians. This separation created a holy lineage for the birth of Christ. Lev. 20:26.

The Old Testament saints like Abraham, Moses and David did not enter the promised land while they were living righteously on this earth, although they looked hopefully for a city whose foundation is Jesus. The separation was consummated after death.

Salvation restores the spiritual life of man which sin destroyed. Cornelius, though a Gentile, was a righteous man, who studied the Word, prayed always and helped the needy. He feared God. Acts 10:1-48. All these good works could not qualify him for the Kingdom and were counted as a memorial to him. God noticed this and sent Peter to go and minister salvation to him so that he would be separated unto God. This would meet God's standard for entrance into Heaven. Please note that God did not decide to put his Name in the book of life because he was reputed to be doing the works of righteousness. Salvation is by grace and standards needed to be met (repentance, faith in Christ, love, water baptism, laying on of hands, Church fellowship). Acts 10:34-35. The mercy of God is perceived in the fact that He noticed his righteousness, and decided to help him. Through the ministration of Peter, he and his household received the gift of the Holy Spirit, Who, through His training, would lead them to Heaven. Ps .32:8. The holy should be separated from the evil, until the due processes of cleansing or deliverance are completed according to the Word of God in 2 Cor. 6:14-18. Separation that is partial creates a different standard. True love, service and self-denial can lose their value in compromise.

Biblical Instances of Separation

The separation of Adam and Eve was from the garden of Eden, the tree of Life and the blessings God had planned for them. These blessings include everlasting life, peace, security, prosperity, fellowship with Him and divine health.

Joshua the High Priest was wearing a dirty garment. The Lord rebuked the devil and commanded his dirty garment, which was blocking his ministry, to be removed. He was separated from his iniquity. Zech. 3:1-10.

Most of us are wearing filthy garments without knowing. Maybe we should cry out to God to reveal to us the garment we are wearing. One day the Lord opened my eyes to behold a white garment I was wearing full of yellow stains. I felt very ashamed. Eccl. 9:8. The process of getting rid of sin is a continuous one. The moment you think you can relax, they can accumulate. I was meant to understand that continuous righteousness is the key. 1 Cor. 10:12.

The legitimate and illegitimate sons of Abraham had to be separated in order to create a clear lineage for the birth of Christ. That separation assumed a sharper distinction in the differences between Christianity and Islam. Abraham, because his foundation was idolatrous, was commanded to move out of his fatherland into an unknown country which God would prepare for him. Gen. 12:1 reads, "Get thee out of thy country, and from thy kindred, and from thy father's house, unto a land that I will show thee." The Lord is still giving this command today, whenever the need arises.

Isaiah saw the glory of God and immediately perceived the need to be separated from sin. Isa. 6:5 reads, "Woe is me for I am undone. For I am a man of unclean lips, and I dwell in the midst of a people of unclean lips. For my eyes have seen the King, the Lord of hosts." Based on his genuine repentance, God ministered immediate separation from sin to him so that He could use him.

Daniel had to separate himself from the defiled food and wine of the Babylonian royalty, although it was sumptuous and tempting. Daniel 1:8.

Moses had to separate himself from the enjoyment of living as the son of the Pharoah's daughter in order to attain an eternal glory based on the truth and will of God for him.

Matt. 5:30 reads, "And if your right hand causes you to sin cut it off and cast it from you; for it is better for you to enter into life maimed rather than having two hands to go to hell, into the fire that shall never be quenched; where their worm does not die, and the fire is not quenched." In the book of Mk. 9:44-48, this injunction was repeated three times with the hands, foot and eyes; Jesus confirming hell fire. Positive separation is so important that one has to ignore the pain that may be attendant to it.

Be Separate from Demons

Eph. 6:12 reads: "For we wrestle not against flesh and blood, but against principalities, against powers, against the rulers of the darkness of this world, against spiritual wickedness in high places."
Demons are invisible disembodied spirits used by Satan to

attack the children of God. They want to live inside human beings. If they are left to remain there, some of them usually cause a lot of harm to their victims. They can be bound and cast out, especially during deliverance sessions or times of serious vigorous prayers. If holiness is not maintained, they return again. Matt. 12:43-45. Demons are responsible for many spiritual and physical disasters, for example mental illness, Matt. 4:23-24, blindness, Matt. 12:22, oppression, Acts 10:38, witchcraft enchantment, Zech. 33:6, epilepsy, Matt. 17:15. They are also responsible for problems like distractions, spiritual sexual assaults, especially those from the water, laziness, irritability, etc. They can degenerate to the depths of bitterness, evil and wickedness by causing great torment or death to their victims. The weapons in Eph. 6:14-18 are to be used against them. Sin creates access for them to get in. This fact reinforces the need to be continually separated from sin. There was a case of a young girl being delivered from demons during a deliverance session. To the amazement of all who were present, the demon spoke and said, "I will go out but tell this girl that if she commits fornication again, I will surely come back." Matt. 12:44. They do not like to be disembodied and resist it. They fear being cast into the lake of fire before the judgement day. Mk. 5:7-8.

It would appear as if Satan has a demon for any sin that

is committed. It is their presence in the body that creates a situation where some of the family members who were friendly suddenly become enemies in the spiritual realm. This is because they are under spiritual manipulations by demons. A mind that is free from demons is a sound mind. Mk. 5:15. The one that is demon-influenced succumbs to demonic influences. Eph. 6:12. A demon-possessed mind has an aspect of his or her life in complete control of demons. This is demonic indwelling. Mk. 5:4.

If you notice that you have done a turnaround from the Word without feeling a remorse in your conscience and the urgent need to repent, do some serious prayers on a continuous basis, using scriptures like the following. Col. 2:14-15; Gal. 3:13-15; Amos 3:3; 2 Cor. 6:14-18; Matt. 15:13; Isa. 49:25-26; Ps. 18:44-45; Ps. 27:2.

The book of 1 Cor. 3:17 went further to state that anyone who defiles the temple of God will be destroyed. If there is anything to be separated from, it is demons. It is the will of God that the holy should be separated from the unholy. All negative influences that can draw people away from God should be avoided. In order to crucify the flesh and walk in the spirit one seriously has to resist the demons who intensify the works of the flesh. God made the means of salvation possible for man through Christ. He made the power or ability to achieve it possible through the Holy

Spirit, Who will guide us on the path of holiness. The demons are aware of this fact and are bitterly contending against it.

The Kingdom is so very precious that Jesus used the parable of the precious expensive pearl, Matt. 13:45, and the parable of the buried treasure to illustrate this. Matt.13:44. If you have to dispose of or separate yourself from everything you own in order to get it, it is worth that sacrifice.

The final day of separation will come on that day that everybody dreads: the day of judgement. Jesus wants us to prepare for that day while we are still alive today. God loves man but hates the sin inside him. He must surely judge sin, which is the common enemy of man because it is in opposition to His divine nature and moral purity. Jon. 12:48 states: "He who rejects Me and does not receive My words has that which judges him. The words that I have spoken will judge him in the last day." In the book of Ezek. 30:15a He said: "I will pour my fury on Sin." In verse 16 He said, "Sin shall have great pain." Unfortunately, sin dwells in the heart of man.

Pray this Prayer Several Times:
O God please let any tree of sin which you did not plant in my body and in my life be uprooted permanently in the Name of Jesus. Matt. 15:13; Ps. 8:44-45.

Chapter Ten

ENDURANCE

"If so be that we suffer with Him, that we may be also glorified together." Rom 8:17b

Christ endured the sin of mankind being placed on his innocent body, in addition to being crucified at the Cross for those sins. Reciprocally man is supposed to endure all that the denial of those sins entails, and to suffer for the sins of others too. How do we endure? 1 Pet. 2:23 reads, "Who when he was reviled did not revile in turn; when he suffered He did not threaten; but committed himself to Him Who judges righteously." Endurance is synonymous to long suffering and like love is connected to all the divine attributes. 1 Cor. 13:4 states, "Love suffers long and is kind." It is kindness that motivates the long suffering. Faith also motivates endurance in the sense that it is the eventual outcome that makes patience possible. Humility is servanthood. You endure the low esteem of this position. In forgiveness you endure the deep hurt and pain that the enemy has brought into your life. In being gentle in your approach, despite serious provocations, you endure the feeling of not retaliating. Lack of endurance gives rise to anxiety and lack of peace. The success of attaining victory through the fruits of the Spirit depends on one's ability to endure. It takes endurance to live a holy and righteous life. Endurance can be defined as a state of always bearing hardship patiently. It is a state of coming to terms with the problems and sufferings of life. It is a willingness to wait patiently for God in unwavering faith in order to achieve what He set out to do in His own time, irrespective of the hardship that one is experiencing. According to the scriptures you endure when you suffer for Christ or for your own sins.

1 Pet. 2:20 makes a definite distinction between suffering for Christ and suffering for one's sins. It reads, "For what glory is it if when ye be buffeted for your faults, ye shall take it patiently? But if when ye do well, and suffer for it ye take it patiently this is acceptable with God." This scripture is saying that God may not necessarily take responsibility for the consequences of man's sins. He is more interested to see man endure persecution as a result of salvation and the Word.

Endurance can be partial; in which case it is done in a half-hearted way with a lot of complaints and shaking of the head. It can be total, which is a complete willingness and surrender to the Word and the Holy Spirit. Heb. 10:36 reads, "For ye have need of patience that after ye have done the Will of God, ye may receive the promise." In order to receive from God one has to wait patiently for Him to unfold His plans at His own time. Perseverance is needed in order to advance in endurance.

The knowledge of the Word, love, faith humility and anointing will not exempt anyone from satanic attacks. Jesus had all these but was not spared from attacks. What is required of us is to reflect the ways of Christ in the way we respond to all these problems. With endurance, one can ignore transgression, and be able to endure all the problems of the evil one victoriously. The end purpose of all the problems that Satan projects is to lead man to sin.
When I faced an unexpected problem, what a divine voice said to me that early morning was that it was the way that I dealt with the problem that is more important than the problem. Col. 3:15. I immediately decided to restrain myself from what I purposed to do and endured and waited patiently for God in prayers. That divine advice glorified God in the end. On another occasion of an unexpected temptation, the divine voice immediately said: "Ignore and move ahead." Jam. 1:2-4 reads, "My brethren count it all joy

when you fall into divers temptations. Knowing this, that the trial of your faith worketh patience." We need patient endurance at the trying of our faith. Endurance cannot come without any trial and temptations; and the Kingdom cannot be entered without much tribulation." Acts 14:22 reads, "...we must through much tribulation enter into the Kingdom of God." What do we endure? Suffering, persecution, affliction, etc. We endure what ordinarily should be resented.

I must confess that certain circumstances do not make this good advice easy to implement. Continuous prayers are needed. I also know that success depends on perseverance, and that adversity is the means to spiritual maturity. Some people wonder why they have to suffer after Christ has taken all that suffering at the Cross. They tend to forget that the one who was and is still responsible for man's sins is still working very hard to bring man down, especially now that he knows that his end is very near. 1 Jon. 3:38. 1 Pet. 5:8 reads, "Be sober, be vigilant; because your adversary the devil works about like a roaring lion, seeking whom he may devour." The Lord is waiting for us to prepare our bodies for Him so that His Spirit can dwell there and lead us on an obedient path to victory. Rom. 12:1 reads, "I beseech you therefore brethren by the mercies of God, that you present your bodies a living sacrifice, holy, acceptable to God which is your reasonable service." This requires a life of endless endurance, determination and perseverance. The Lord is our strength, and we prevail by exercising faith in His ability to lead us by His Spirit, blameless to the Kingdom.

Rom. 8:17-18 reads, "If so be that we suffer with him, that we may also be glorified together. For I reckon that the sufferings of the present time are not worthy to be compared with the glory which shall be revealed to us." The benefits outweigh the present hardship. Endure without complaint so that you can avoid sin. If you think you can no longer endure and as a result stop seeking God, He may stop attending to you and may leave you alone altogether. In Jon. 8:29 Jesus Himself said, "And He Who sent Me is with Me. The Father has not left Me alone, for I always do those things that please Him." He endured till death. Ordinary humans like us ought then to be extremely careful.

Do you know the extent to which one should endure? Heb. 12:4-6 reads, "Ye have not yet resisted unto blood striving against sin. And ye have not forgotten the exhortation which speaketh unto you as unto children. My son, despise not thou the chastening of the Lord, nor faint when thou art rebuked by Him. For whom the Lord loveth He chasteneth, and scourgeth every son whom He receiveth." Scourging is the acceptable divine discipline of God.

Endurance Through Faith

Faith is the strength of God in our lives that makes it possible for us to patiently, pass through temptations and afflictions in the world. Endurance makes the walk of faith possible. When God makes a promise, it is only through faith and endurance that one can wait for its fulfilment. The Word states that His strength makes perfect our weaknesses. 2 Cor.12:9. This makes endurance possible. We present our weaknesses looking up to Him, believing that He is able to put everything right; and because of this we keep enduring. Jesus said we should forgive each other forty-nine times seven. It takes a lot of endurance to do this. Christian believers are expected to perceive suffering as a regular phenomenon and an inevitable part of Christian life. Faith can move God to make the temptations always endurable.

In the book of 1 Pet. 5:10 it is stated that after you have endured, He will establish, perfect, strengthen and settle you. Maintaining a spirit of endurance is so important that, as mentioned earlier, Christ advised that if your endurance level would establish the need to endure the pain of plucking off the eye or cutting off the hand in order to avoid sin, you should go ahead and do so. Matt. 5:29-30.

Biblical Examples of Some Who Endured:

Abraham

Although regarded as the father of faith he is also the father of endurance. There cannot be found among mankind anyone whose faith, patience and endurance can be compared to that of Abraham. He waited for over ten years for the promise of a son, although he was not far from a hundred years in age. This is because he knew the God he was serving. Acts 5:29 reads, "We ought to obey God rather than men." He was living in tents, moving from one place to the other, waiting patiently for God to position him in the promised land. God asked him to move away from his foundation.

Very few people will agree to turn their backs on their relatives who do not pose a physical threat to their lives. Some will demand their own share of inheritance before leaving their fatherland. When God asked Abraham in Gen. 12:1-5 to move from his fatherland finally for a new land, his obedience was instant, because of his deeply rooted faith in God. He encountered a lot of difficulties in the process of doing this. He never went back but endured all the tribulations he encountered willingly, including threats to his life. At the age of ninety-nine years God confirmed the promise that his seed shall come from Sarah, his wife, not from Ishmael whom he had at the age of eighty-six. He believed, and it was accounted to him for righteousness. He also had to wait for over ten years before this happened. Waiting requires a lot of endurance.

Paul

Paul is another father of endurance; before his conversion he made many suffer for their faith. After his conversion he did not allow any form of suffering to be a hindrance to his calling. In Acts 9:16 Jesus said, "For I will show him many great things he will suffer for My Name's sake." He already knew what Paul would encounter and so strengthened him. God allowed chastening for those He loved. Paul went through many physical afflictions joyfully without any complaint and gave glory to God for everything. In 2 Cor. 11:24-27 he made a summary of all his afflictions and sufferings. Many of them were life threatening, but he did not perish in any of them because his faith in God kept him alive. According to the psalmist in Ps. 34:19, God kept all his bones intact, not one of them was broken. When anyone begins to question why afflictions, persecutions and sufferings should arise, the person has missed the whole point of salvation. Christians should regard them as evidence of their love for Christ, who passed through worse agony and pain and is a perfect example of endurance.

Joseph

(Gen. 37:12-30; 40:1-23, 45:1-6) Joseph endured the heartache of being betrayed by his own brothers, who also had wanted to kill him. He loved and trusted them, but they hated him and wanted him out of the way. In the book of Matt. 10:36 Jesus said, "And a man's enemies will be those of his own household." He revealed his dreams to his enemies. Once when it would appear as if I was revealing my secrets, a divine voice cautioned: "Secret things should be kept secret." Pro. 11:13. He endured life in chains in prison for the offence he did not commit. In spite of all these he refused to doubt God. God was with him and made him emerge victorious.

Daniel, Shadrach, Meshach, and Abednego

We are familiar with Daniel's case in the lion's den and how King Darius was convicted. He immediately passed a decree acknowledging that the God of Daniel is the living God. Dan. 6:25-27. Shadrach, Meshach and Abednego decided to endure being in a flaming fire despite the threat of being burnt to death. Dan. 3:25. The King was convicted and blessed the God of Shadrach, Meshach and Abednego. All these dramatic acts of suffering became possible as a result of faith and the determination to endure.

The Greatest Lesson in Endurance

Jesus's endurance covered every aspect of human affliction and woe and exceeded it. He, the Living Word through Whom God spoke life to the world and mankind, left His divine form, condescending to take the form of man. He endured patiently and willingly the role of a humble servant of man. Matt. 20:28. In his unjust affliction and torture, they spat at, mocked and slapped Him and put a reed on His Head. After that they pushed a crown of thorns on His Head, calling Him King of the Jews. He opened not His mouth. At that time of loneliness, He experienced the burden of human sin and the abandonment of God, for God's eyes do not behold sin. Isa. 53:4b reads, "Yet we esteemed Him stricken, smitten by God and afflicted." His suffering was part of God's providential plan for man. If God did not spare the sin placed on the innocent body of Christ, is it the ones on our sinful bodies that He will spare? We pray that God will give us the understanding to endure the denial of all sins in Jesus's Name.

Isa. 53:7-8 reads, "He was oppressed and He was afflicted. Yet He opened not His Mouth. He was led as a lamb to the slaughter, and as a sheep before its shearers is silent. So, He opened not His mouth. He was denied justice." He endured crucifixion.

Chapter Eleven

THE WAY OF JOY

"My brethren count it all joy when ye fall into diverse temptations; knowing this, that the trying of your faith worketh patience." Jam. 1:2-3

Jon. 15:11 reads, "These things I have spoken to you, that My joy may remain in you, and that your joy may be full." The way to the fullness of joy is Christlikeness. Only through the grace of God can this be made possible. Jesus asked His disciples to pray that His joy may be full in them in order that they might attain Christlikeness. Joy is a fruit of the spirit, and it is required of every believer to dwell in joy despite all adverse circumstances.

Isa. 35:10 reads, "And the ransomed of the Lord shall return. And come to Zion with songs, and everlasting joy upon their heads. They shall obtain joy and gladness, and sorrow and sighing shall flee away." Literally this passage refers to the return of the Israelites from captivity to their own land. It also refers in the present to the return of the redeemed to God. The thought of this has been a source of joy to them all this while. Rejoicing makes the journey to the Kingdom easier. Sorrow is the opposite of joy, and is contrary to faith.

The Christian journey is not always sorrowful when undertaken with the right attitude of mind, with faith and joy. Ps. 16:11 confirms this. It reads, "In His presence is fullness of joy, at His right Hand are pleasures for evermore." In Lk. 10:17, 21, Jesus made His disciples understand that the whole purpose of joy is based on the hope of salvation in the end. When you always focus on God's promises in the end and turn every situation into that of joy, it is very rewarding. The fact that one is saved and is on the way to the Kingdom should be a continuous source of happiness and joy.

Christ Jesus was our living example of joy in a difficult situation as stated earlier. Heb. 12:2 reads, "Looking unto Jesus the Author and Finisher of our faith, Who for the joy that was set before Him endured the Cross, despising the shame, and has sat down at the right hand of the throne of God." He was able to do this because He continually set His Mind on the positive outcome of His mission on this earth. In Matt. 5:11-12 Jesus said, "Blessed are ye when men shall revile you and persecute you, and say all manner of evil against you falsely for my sake. Rejoice and be exceedingly glad for great is your reward in heaven." Joy is a sacrifice and, like other sacrifices, requires some self-denial; for example, the denial of pain, anger and worry leads to joy. Sometimes when serious problems arise, we tend to wonder how to accommodate joy. I usually resort to prayers for with God all things are possible. By the time you complete that prayer the feeling of anger has either gone or eased off tremendously. Pray for the enabling power of the Holy Spirit to take captive the thoughts of your heart. Every believer has to fight the battle of the mind in order to be able to focus the mind on joyful things and the Word. When Christ increases in you, your joy also is increased. This section will briefly discuss some of the requirements that may make this increase possible.

Acts 17:28 states, "In Him we live, move and have our being." This is Christlikeness in the way we think, speak and act. Every likeness of Christ in our lives indicates a closer move towards Heaven and gives cause for joy. This joy will motivate us to move closer to His likeness. One wonders how many of us are really interested in striving to live this way. Phil. 2:2 reads, "Fulfil my joy by being like-minded, having the same love, being of one accord, of one mind." This is the unity of Christlikeness.

One way of making this increase possible is having a good knowledge of the Word, knowing His likes and dislikes. 2 Pet. 3:18 reads, "But grow in the grace and knowledge of our Lord and Saviour Jesus Christ. It is from the Word that you will learn God's reactions to human failures that are often taken for granted. Christ is the Word, and if you develop a mastery of the Word Christ has increased in you and you will experience His fullness of joy. Jon. 1:14.

Christlikeness, which brings joy, cannot increase in you if you are out of communication with Him through prayers. Prayers invite the Triune into our lives. The Holy Spirit in Rom. 8:25-26 intercedes for us in a language which only God can understand. The Lord Jesus Christ is our Great High Priest, Who presents the petitions and requests before God. 1 Tim. 2:5. As we continue in dialogue with God in our prayers we grow in confidence and faith. Faith motivates not only obedience but joy. We are aware that without the help of the Holy Spirit the fullness of joy will not be possible since joy is one of His fruits. In 1 Thess. 1:6, Paul talks of receiving the Word with much affliction and the joy of the Holy Spirit. The Spirit of God is Holy and operates in an atmosphere of joy and contentment, and not of irritation, anger and hatred.

Christlikeness encourages the expectation of reward and joy in the end. Obedience and holiness are major conditions that determine its growth. Faith encourages it. It is by the grace of God that one can consistently abide in joy, and it is necessary to continue to ask for this grace.

2 Cor. 6:16-17 reads, "And what agreement has the temple of God with idols? For you are the temple of the living God. As God has said: "Come out from among them, and be separate says the Lord. Do not touch what is unclean and I will receive you. I will be a Father to you, and you shall be my sons and daughters, says the Lord almighty." This emphasises the need to keep away from things that detract from His likeness. We are created in the image of God and His form depicts perfect holiness. In Gen. 1:26 God in His love and humility said: "Let Us make man in Our image, according to Our likeness." This likeness needs to be preserved in awe and fear of Him since our bodies are temples of His Spirit. If we allow our bodies to be defiled by living a morally depraved life or eating food used in occultic practices etc., we lose the Christlikeness, unless we repent genuinely. Without repentance any joy we feel is not of the Lord. According to Ps. 139, we are "fearfully and wonderfully made" so that we can reflect this joy. In the book of Daniel 1:8, Daniel refused to eat the King of Babylon's delicacies of food and his wine. This was because

he suspected that it might have been dedicated to false gods. He never lost his anointing for wisdom, knowledge and understanding, vision and prophecy, which is Christlike.

The Decrease of the Flesh

When we grow in the spirit we are doing so in the likeness of Christ, who is the perfect likeness of God. According to Jon. 3:30, "He must increase but I must decrease." The Spirit must grow as the flesh is crucified. Jon. 6:63. Jesus said that it is the spirit that quickens and the flesh profits nothing. The flesh with its carnality is passing away, but the spiritual and the heavenly will remain. It is the spiritual that gives everlasting joy. Most of us are spiritually not alive, and need Christ to resurrect us back to life. God is a spirit and needs us to relate to Him spiritually and not through the flesh.

In Jon. 11:25 Jesus said to the Samaritan woman at the well, whose moral was not clear: "God is a Spirit and those who worship Him must worship in the Spirit and in truth." The truth that comes from a sincere and humble heart is Christlike. That woman attained an immediate spiritual growth and became an evangelist. Out of joy and excitement she forgot her pitcher of water and rushed to go and bring people to Christ. The increase of Christ in the life of a believer is perceptible in his character and behaviour. If you are lacking in faith, Christ will not increase in you because you have placed that faith in something or somebody else. The Law was a preparation for this faith in Christ that gives joy and everlasting life. Man was saved by grace through faith. Eph. 2:8.

If you are proud, Christ will not increase in you, because God will know you from a far distance. If you belong to a Church and have not experienced any spiritual growth, maybe you have not decreased appreciably in order to allow Him to increase in you. If you are the type that is more concerned about how the world perceives you, it is the world that is increasing in you; that is being worldly and not Christlike. If your actions are always motivated by your friends or a particular individual, then it is the control of these people that are increasing in you and hindering the joy of the Lord. These are manifestations of idolatry in different forms as a result of misplaced faith and does not motivate joy. It was the Jezebelic doctrine that increased in Ahab. It is what is always in the heart that increases. If you are only interested in doing what is convenient and interesting, it is the joy of the flesh that is increasing. Alternatively, if your actions are seriously based on the Word of God because you know that such will glorify God, you are getting to the fullness of Christ and His joy.

Chapter Twelve

— THE HIDDEN ERRORS —

"Be sober, be vigilant; because your adversary the devil, as a roaring lion, walketh about, seeking whom he may devour." 1 Pet. 5:8

The purpose of being reminded of these errors is not to be critical but to be reminded of some imperfections often taken for granted by some, including me. These errors seriously hinder the move to get there.

Lack of Aggressive Prayer Method

1 Cor. 10:13 states, "There hath no temptation overtaken you, but such as is common to man; But God is faithful, who will not suffer you to be tempted above that you are able; but will with the temptation also make the way of escape, that you may be able to bear it." There are some who are of the impression that their faith in Christ is strong, having all the fruits of the Holy Spirit or so it would

appear. They seem happy and content. But immediately a persistent serious temptation arises, and a lot of prayers has been offered about it, if no answer is forthcoming, they tend to develop a little fear and doubt. At this stage the evil one can push anxiety and irritability into such a heart. We know that the Holy Spirit does not operate in an atmosphere of anxiety, fear and irritability. It may even be that a greater faith and a more aggressive prayer warfare is required in order to get through. Knocking can be added to asking as in Matt. 7:7. Isa. 66:8 reads, "For as soon as Zion was in labour, she gave birth to her children."

We are told that as we labour spiritually in our prayers, we are more likely to receive answers from God, all conditions being fulfilled. What I usually do before labouring, is to review the specified biblical conditions for answered prayers and how I responded to them and also to pray continuously against the spirit of anxiety and fear. Remember that Jesus was sweating blood when He prayed at Gethsemane. Remember that Elijah prayed several times over with all his strength before rain came back. 1 Kings 18:41-45. Remember that Hezekiah agonised laboriously in prayer before God reversed His decision of death. 2 Kings. 20:1-11. While waiting, intensify your work for God, be it evangelism or intercession. The scripture says rend your heart and not your garment. Joel 2:13. Moreover, God's ways are not the same as ours.

Provision and Reward

A more specific area of inconsistency is on finance and reward. As a believer you are doing well, believing God that a labourer is worthy of his pay. Sometimes God may like to test your loyalty to Him. He may decide to withhold your financial supply for a while. You have noticed that the money is not forthcoming as usual, but you are standing on faith, believing that God will restore the usual provision. But after a couple of years, you decide to do something for yourself. You begin to indirectly ask for money from people you prayed for on the basis that a labourer is worthy of his own pay and forgetting Christ's words. They, believing that they are blessing a man of God, will indirectly begin to pay for the prayers they receive. In Matt. 10:8, Jesus said, "Freely ye have, freely ye give." There is need to persist in faith instead of doing it your own way. Jesus never gave up on anything He started. Ps. 138:8; Phil. 1:6; 1 Pet. 5:10. God will give you the grace to manage the hardship until an alternative provision is made. He can also release a creative blessing for you.

Authoritative Leadership

In this type of leadership, things have been so programmed

that decision making is unilateral and not sometimes based on leadership consultation. In the Christian set-up, which is based on the life of Christ and the Word, we are meant to understand that it is not how we lead, but how we serve others that matters. A good Christian leader is characterised by a humble attitude and a servant-like devotion aimed at alleviating the problems of others. He is free from self-centred presumptions and open to conviction, correction and change. He is no respecter of persons; ready to learn even from those below him or her. In Lk. 22:26 Jesus said to His disciples who were wondering who would be the leader among them: "But ye shall not be so, but he that is greatest among you let him be as the younger, and he that is chief as he that doth serve."

False Promise

Promises are made to many people that prayers will continue to be made for them. They base their hope on the fact that these prayers will be made. Unfortunately, the one who gave this assurance encounters serious delays and hindrances and as a result only briefly does the prayers or forgets to do some. I must confess that I encountered a similar problem year back, and a divine messenger warned me not to deceive people. This error comes under the sin of omission in Jam. 4:17. "To him who knows to do good and does not do it to him it is sin." God have mercy on us all.

Concealing the Truth

The Holy Spirit can give you an insight or a way out of a difficult situation based on the Word. You are aware that this insight will in no small measure be of benefit to many. Rather than revealing it to as many as possible, which He really will want you to do as a good minister of God, you whisper or reveal it only to favourites. The easiest way of getting it across is to tell the man of God if he is the type that is receptive to such messages. The Word of God in Deut. 29:29 reads, "The secret things belong to the Lord our God, but those things which are revealed belong to us and to our children forever, that we may do all the words of this law. This is the reason behind the revelation. The application of a message from God is universal. In Hos. 4:6 God Himself said, "My people are destroyed because of lack of knowledge. Because you have rejected knowledge, I also will reject you from being priest for me." God is no respecter of persons. Everybody has to strive in order to avoid this pitfall of sin.

Vain Glory

Do not be carried away by vain glory. This may be as a result of pride in success. You have grown because you sought Him first before all else. He as a result fulfilled His covenant promise of His Word in your life by blessing you beyond measure. But He blessed you so that you will be a blessing to others. The Word of God in Jon. 3:30 states: "He must increase, but I must decrease." In poverty and in wealth one can still decrease as Christ increases. A sacrificial life of forbearance and self-control and obedience is of great help in this situation. The fact that one commands demons to come out and they obey cannot qualify anybody for the Kingdom. In Luke 10:20 Jesus said to His disciples: "Nevertheless, do not rejoice in this, that the spirits are subject to you, but rather rejoice because your names are written in heaven."

Area Called

You are happy because you are a branch pastor or a minister of the Word. You did not know that the plan of God for your life was different, and that He called you for the children's ministry. This may be because you did not take time to wait on Him to find out what He destined for you. I was trained as a pastor and sent out with other pastors to go and train aspiring pastors in the Church. I spent some time seeking the face of the Lord about the spiritual difficulties I was facing where there should be none at all. Then one night He said to me, "I did not call you to pastor. You missed your destiny. I called you for evangelism." He also mentioned a second area which I prefer to keep to myself for the time being. A prominent man of God was always saying repeatedly in his sermons that any time spent in an area that is not your calling is a wasted effort and time. We pray for the mercy of God in order to avoid this mistake.

Unteachability

We as believers are being trained in the school of the Holy Spirit. This training will only end when we leave this world. Due to circumstances and spiritual level, people are at different stages of the training. Faith, discipline and obedience are necessary for the success of this training. Ps. 32:8-9 reads, "I will instruct thee and teach thee in the way which thou shalt go. I will guide thee with My eye. Be ye not as the horse or the mull which have no understanding, whose mouth must be held in with bit and bridle, lest they come near unto you." We are required to develop a sharp sensitivity to this training and live in expectation of it. The scripture in Isa. 26:3 says, "He keepeth him in perfect peace, whose mind is stayed on Him, because he trusted in Him." The distractions in the world, individual circumstances, the flesh and its lusts do not make this requirement easy. Teachability demands careful attention to what the Holy Spirit is saying to us in the scriptures so that we can grow and mature spiritually.

Taking the Blood for Granted

Many people must have made this mistake when they were newly born again. This is being of the mistaken impression that the new birth is only forgiveness of sins, and that this forgiveness is automatic. Also, that the blood is available under any condition. A divine voice once asked me a question: "Felicia, how would you feel if somebody kept asking you for forgiveness every time?" I felt sorry for myself because it meant that the person was a habitual sinner and had not genuinely repented; and that person was me. Titus 2:14.

The blood of Christ is of perfect purity, and it was released with complete purity, love, willingness, a lot of excruciating pain, agony and humiliation. The blood is true to its quality, and it demands love, faith purity and truth in its application. This fact enhances its power in the life of believers. If we want this blood to operate in our lives, then we need to plead it in faith, love and in the truth of the Word. 2 Cor. 12:9 reads, "My grace is sufficient unto thee and My strength makes perfect your weakness." We know that grace threads on righteousness and the strength of God comes by faith. We walk in faith when we walk in obedience to the instructions of God in our lives. Under the new wine skin of the blood of Jesus we add righteousness and not the old one of unrighteousness for its application.

Lack of Unity

The Holy Spirit weaves the web of unity in the hearts of believers. Disunity goes with lack of love and faith. The Lord once asked me to pray for love and unity in the Church. The roots of disunity in the Church can be traced to pride, race, gender, money, education and level of spiritual development. One would think that in the body of Christ the unity as of God the Father, Son and the Holy Spirit should be a way of life. Unfortunately, in some Churches, this is still not so. Gal. 3:26-28 reads: "For ye are all the children of God by faith in Christ Jesus. For as many of you as have been baptised into Christ have put on Christ. There is neither Jew nor Greek, there is neither bond nor free, there is neither male nor female, for ye are all one in Christ Jesus. And if you are Christ's then you are Abraham's seed, and heirs according to the promise." This quotation speaks for itself. The unity of faith should be regarded as sacred. The agents of disunity spend time and thought to find excuses to put away God's choices in His Body. God's election is by grace, and He will cut the number short by righteousness. The Gentiles also were welcomed into the house of God in the apostolic days.

Most Churches have sorted out the issue of gender in line with the scriptural practices. Paul worked with Priscilla and Aquila, Acts 18:1-3, 26. Deborah was a prophetess and a Judge in Israel in the Old Testament. Anna the prophetess witnessed to the Child Jesus when he was brought into the temple to be presented to the Lord. The four daughters of Philip were prophetesses. Jesus respected and appreciated the help of women in His ministry. He drew out their potentials for His work, like the Samaritan woman He met at the well and converted into an evangelist. There are presently the gates of Hades in some Churches hindering unity. In Matt. 16-18 Jesus said, "On this rock I will build My Church and the gates of Hades shall not prevail against it." The Words of Christ are always Amen.

Partial Forgiveness

You may call it partial forgiveness, but to the Lord it is still unforgiveness. When reference is continually made to a matter that has been forgiven, it makes the forgiveness questionable. It is advisable that we stop making reference to it, however deep the hurt is. I did not at first realise this. Something happened many years back. One day the effect of this weakness suddenly came on me in the form of a multitude of problems. I frantically cried out to God in the following words: "Lord, where are you?" Immediately His Voice answered: "The problem of those who do not forgive is that their malaise is like a cankerworm that eats through their entire bodies. Forgive and let it go." Eph. 4:32.

What I did was to start praying for those who hurt me. I realised that in fact they are under the instigation of the evil one and not aware of the consequences of their actions. This made me feel sympathetic and forgiving towards them.

Fear of Death and Hell

Scripturally, genuine, born again Christians should not be afraid of death since they are supposed to know where they are going. One of the courses I attended in the Bible College was on Discipleship and Mission. This was over twenty years ago. I really enjoyed the sensitivity of it. One day the lecturer asked those who were not afraid to die to indicate by raising their hands. I found that I was the only one who raised a hand. I did not do so because I wanted to die, far from it. I just wanted to clarify a point based on that question. I pointed out that it was not necessarily the time of death that causes great concern to Christians but the destination after death. Somebody whom God recalled in order to be put in Heaven is incomparably better than the one who died at the age of a hundred and was cast into Hell. It is the fear of our destination that should also motivate one's behaviour in this world. Rom. 8:2.

Misuse of Anointing

It is only the grace of God that can enable an anointed

believer to continue to operate in humility, faith and love. Sometimes anointing can be subject to abuse through pride or quest for money. Anointing is for the work of God. It is not an indication of entrance into Heaven. Although it is from God, any continuous misuse of it can attract any discipline from God. It can be abused when the anointed is attributing its power to self which is stealing the glory of God, when used to terminate life, hinder God's progress for man or to negate God's directives about its use. The necessary restraint should be exercised.

About eighteen years ago when I was ministering to a group of women seeking God's face for the fruit of the womb; because things were happening, I just kept laying hands on them indiscriminately. Then the directives came. "From this time if you have to lay hands on anybody both of us have to do it." He has to give the permission. On another occasion, I laid hands on another without just asking Him. For many years, I really suffered for this error. It is only recently that I got a comforting assurance. 1 Tim. 5:22 reads, "Do not lay hands on anyone hastily, nor share in other people's sins; keep yourself pure."

Chapter Thirteen

- THE SPIRIT OF BACKWARDNESS -

"No man having put his hand in the plough, and looking back is fit for the Kingdom of God." Lk. 9:62

The perception of a state of backwardness can be hazy. One may be moving backwards but think that they are really moving forward. Scripturally the Spirit of backwardness is contrary to any growth in faith. The rich young ruler of Matt. 19:16-24 got to a stage of growth when he started moving backwards. He was convinced that he was moving forwards until Christ spoke to him. He made Christ understand that he had kept all the commandments since he was a child. Christ in His compassionate and encouraging way was impressed but informed him that there was just one thing that he needed to do: to dispose of all his wealth and follow Him. This was because his thoughts were on his acquisitions; how to preserve and maybe make them grow. This would not allow him to completely give his heart to God. He did not welcome the idea of getting rid of his wealth, which had become his idol. Matt. 6:24 reads: "You cannot serve God and mammon." In Rev. 3:1-6, Jesus made the Church in Sardis who thought that they were moving forward in victory to understand that they were far from that conception. He said: "I know your works, that you have a name, that you are alive, but you are dead."

The spirit of backwardness can turn a wilderness experience into a nightmare. If a believer that has received the Holy Spirit baptism still continues to live in any known sin, that person will be moving backwards spiritually. Growth in the Word, living one's faith and prayers war against backwardness. If the destination of this backward movement is not halted, it can lead to apostasy. In Lk. 9:62 Christ warned against this spirit: "And Jesus said unto them, no man having put his hand to the plough and looking back, is fit for the Kingdom of God." Backwardness is a major cause of backsliding.

Some Reasons for Backwardness

Procrastination
This is a habit that allows good opportunities to slip away. It can be said to be one of the main reasons for

backwardness. It is the flesh that suggests that one should take a break, and easily suggests another rest when you are about to get up. It is the flesh that pushes one to put aside a particular assignment for another less important one. It is the eyes working in conjunction with the flesh that detects any distraction first. The scripture in Eph. 5:15-16 advises, "See then that you walk circumspectly, not as fools but as wise; redeeming the time because the days are evil." This is a serious call not to waste any time available and not to spend it on irrelevant matters. If you spend your time observing with your eyes what is considered useless for spiritual growth, you will be moving backwards, not forward. Going forward is moving in the light of the gospel, while ignorance of the Word signifies darkness which means backward movement.

Matt. 6:22-23 reads, "The lamp of the body is the eye. If therefore your eye is good, your whole body will be full of light. But if your eye is bad, your whole body will be full of darkness." The good eye is moving forward while the evil eye is moving backwards.

The Abuse of Money

The abuse of money, especially in the house of God, attracts backwardness. The book of 2 Cor. 8:9 states that

Jesus became poor, so that through His poverty believers will become rich. In other words that believers through imitating His forbearance and self-giving may receive the richness of His grace. Unfortunately, some of us are being distracted by the spirit of self-seeking and covetousness. 2 Cor. 9:8 has given the assurance that God will always provide the grace that will attract enough financial benefit in order to do His work.

Financial obligations are explained in Lk. 6:34 and in Mal. 3:10-11. Withholding the tithe brings backwardness. One is also required to pay first fruit offering. It is also very advisable to sow a seed of faith as the need arises. This fact is explained in Gen. 8:22 and Eccl. 11:4. "In the morning sow thy seed, and in the evening withhold not thy hand." This means that you should not hesitate over whether it will be a worthwhile venture or not because it is God Who will make it grow. Man is supposed to apply the same discipline of living the fruits of the Spirit to his or her attitude towards money so that it does not control him. One's attitude towards money can be a reflection of the person's love for God.

Some years back I decided to borrow some money from

the tithe I was to pay into the Church because I felt that God was the only one Who would understand. It had not dawned on me that He never changes His Word. In my prayers I let Him know that the reason for such an action was that I felt it was better and safer to borrow from Him than from a human being. After this, things got really bad for me financially, in spite of the fact that I was praying over this regularly. He had always provided for my needs. I then decided to politely ask Him what was going on with my finances. Immediately I uttered the last word of the prayers, an emphatic answer came. "You cannot withhold a tithe." Deut. 14:22. I was one of the earliest customers at the bank the next morning. Much later when I needed some financial provision and prayed about it, a voice asked in the spirit realm: "Is she owing anything?" The person to whom the question was directed answered "No."

The evil one is continually fighting against the finances of believers because he knows that their first expenditure is to pay their tithes. Christian brethren are advised to fulfil all financial obligations in the Church so that no doorway will be left open for the evil one.

Untreated Foundation

This is a major cause of backwardness. An evil foundation will always put hindrances on any forward move you make in order to destroy your destiny. If it fails in this, it will try to destroy you. At the spiritual forefront of your foundation are the ancestral spirits whose aims are to control and manipulate members of the family for their evil purposes, just the way they did to their forefathers who unfortunately rendered idolatrous services to them. If one does not have the spirit of Christ, the person can easily succumb to their threats either consciously or unconsciously. God did not give believers the spirit of fear but of power, love and a sound mind.

These foundational enemies are the trees Jesus referred to in Matt. 15:13. The Word in 1 Cor. 3:11 reads, "For no other foundation can anyone lay than that which is laid, which is Jesus Christ." In Matt. 10:36 Jesus pointed out the fact that a man's enemies shall be those of his own household. The household enemies are motivated by the ancestral and evil spirits from the foundation. The Word of God in Jon. 10:10 tells us that they come to steal, kill and to destroy, but that Jesus has come that we might have life and have it more abundantly. Whenever the move of Jesus through the Holy

Spirit comes into conflict with the extreme wickedness of these enemies, a family spiritual warfare develops as members support opposing factions. This is what Matt. 10:34-36 is all about. Aggressive spiritual conflict through prayers, utilising all the weapons of warfare which God has made available to believers in Eph. 6:12-18, becomes an immediate necessity.

One family member may be a believer, who spends time in the Word, prayers and fasting, and in the work of the Lord, while also trying to come to terms with the rebuff and spiritual attacks of opposing members. Another one who has developed a spiritual relationship with the kingdom of darkness can fly off in the night to her meetings and narrate all the secret information from the family. Mic. 5-6 reads, "Do not trust in a friend; do not put your confidence in a companion; guard the doors of your mouth from her who lies in your bosom." It is all as a result of an evil foundation. A family foundation that is sincerely standing on the rock of Christ will not separate family members." It is the enemy who is very knowledgeable about you who will effectively hinder you from getting there. Satan uses these close enemies to make getting there a difficult process. The book of Matt. 10:34-36 should not be literally interpreted to mean that the gospel only brings divisions in the family. Christ said in Jon. 14:27, "Peace I leave with you. My peace I give unto you; not as the world giveth give I unto you." From this passage it can be seen that Christ is the arbiter of peace. What this passage means is that the result of walking successfully on the rough and narrow way is the reward and peace it guaranties in the end. There is need to cry out to God continually in fasting and prayers for deliverance from an evil foundation.

Dreams

The worst agent of backwardness is the dream. It is where the forces of darkness programme what happens in people's lives. It can be called the theatre on which the ancestral spirits act out their evil plans. It is the central area where people's steps are reversed from their destiny.

It is very important to remember your dreams so that you will know what to present to God in prayers when you wake up. If you lose an important possession or encounter a defeat in the dream through any form of attack, and by the time you wake up have forgotten all about it, it means that the enemy may have an upper hand against a particular area of your life. On waking up if one remembers a bad dream, it is advisable to immediately cry out to God in prayers to cancel or reverse it. Scriptures like Col. 2:14; Matt. 15:13; Isa. 54:15; Rom. 8:2 and Ps. 27:2 can prove helpful in such situations.

It is also in the dream that the enemy projects spiritual substitutes of husbands, wives, children, etc. and makes them act out their parts. One can also be manipulated into secret covenants. These evil spiritual operations can lead to financial reverses, failure at the edge of miracles, demonic delays of progress, accidents, constant marital problems, delayed pregnancies and strange sicknesses. Strong prayers before sleep is necessary. By obeying the will of God, one gets the Holy Spirit to defeat the plans of the enemy. Some of the problems experienced by people can have their roots traced to what goes on in the dreams.

Misplaced Destiny

There is always a destiny for specific assignments by God for those He called, apart from the general call to preach the gospel in Mk. 16:15, and to pray for the sick in Jam. 5:16. The enemy has a way of manipulating people away from the area that God has called them. If one is operating in an area not called, this is a spiritual diversion from the original plan of God for that life. Sometimes the mistake may be unintentional, or because one never made time to enquire sufficiently from Him.

This fact establishes the need to enquire from the Lord firstly in order to determine the area He destined for one. The call can come through different ways. Through prayers or laying on of hands as in the case of Timothy, or that of Paul and Barnabas in Acts 13:2 when the Holy Spirit spoke out. It can also come by a direct encounter like Paul on the way to Damascus. In Matt. 7:7 Jesus said: "Ask and it will be given to you."

Wrong Names

Some names have evil meanings which impact negatively on the character of the one bearing it. Some have given their children names derived from that of ancient gods and goddesses. Helen is derived from Helena. Ordinarily they are perceived as normal and prestigious but spiritually can influence one's behaviour. Though given with good intention it can mean an initiation through ignorance.

The name Linda means snake. In Gen. 32:28 the angel who wrestled with Jacob changed his name from Jacob to Israel. Jacob stands for a supplanter or deceiver. Israel means Prince of God or may God persevere. He had to be delivered by that angel from the spirit of supplanting. His mother had forced him to deceive both his father and his brother. In Gen. 32:28 Laban, his maternal uncle, played back his deceit on him. God changed his name and things changed for him. When a divine voice shouted at me to change my name, I did not waste time to do it. I had for a long time been trying to determine the meaning of the name.

In Gen. 17:5 God said to Abraham, "Neither shall thy name anymore be called Abram, but thy name shall be Abraham; for I have made you a father of many nations." In verse 15 God said, "As for Sarai your wife you shall not call her name Sarai, but Sarah shall be her name." This change was necessary in order to incorporate her into the new covenant. In 1 Sam. 4:21 the daughter-in-law of Eli, at the news of the death of her husband and father-in-law, and the capture of the Ark by the Philistines, had a precipitated labour and was delivered of a baby boy. She named the child Ichabod. This name means that the glory had departed from Israel. She acted in ignorance of the future implications of the name based on the unfortunate circumstances at the time of the boy's birth. The scripture made us to understand that the boy cried out desperately to God to change his name when things did not work out well for him. God in His mercy answered his prayers.

In Africa, Ibo names like Nwosu, Adaora and Nnamdi need to be seriously examined before they are given to children. One also has to examine the new surname that they have by marriage. Some names are also good. Dan means praise or thanksgiving. Joseph means He will enlarge. Benjamin means to exalt or honour.

The Evil One

The evil one is largely responsible for the spirit of backwardness. Once the power of the Holy Spirit moves in a life, the evil one will immediately make a desperate move to oppose this. Once God gives you a serious instruction of what to do, the evil one will come up with all the reasons why you have to disobey that instruction. If you pray hard and the enemy is defeated and God releases a breakthrough, you will still have to pray hard in order to retain it. This is why the psalmist said in Psalm 69:4b, "That which I did not steal I must restore."

Chapter Fourteen

— THE HOLY SPIRIT —

"But ye shall receive power after that the Holy Ghost is come upon you; and ye shall be witnesses unto Me." Acts. 1:8

Righteousness can only be achieved through the leading of the Holy Spirit, because it is He Who can bring about newness of heart in humans. He prepares the hearts of believers for the Kingdom. His fruits characterise the righteousness of God. In the Old Testament the people did not have this benefit of His, because Christ had not died and risen. His anointing was reserved for the spiritual and national leaders. But in the new covenant every believer is required to receive it and become a priest and a king. All Christians should ask for a supply of the Holy Spirit in order to be transformed to the Christlike way. If you are baptised by immersion and have not received this free gift, continue to ask for it. It is our responsibility to retain Him inside our hearts through obedience to the will of God. A body without the Spirit is scripturally dead and not useful to God. If you defile your body He can decide to step aside until genuine repentance comes. He guides us on the plan of God for our lives. Ps. 32:8. Like Jesus He has the same purpose, plan and power with God the Father. He is the one who helps us to pray to the Father. Rom. 8:26-27. Eph. 2:18 reads, "For through Him we both have access by one Spirit to God the Father." He stands for a united body of believers. The Church is the Spiritual Body of Christ and all believers are united in spirit with each other and with God. He imparts the likeness of Christ and the love of God into the hearts of believers. Those who are led by the Spirit of God (who obey His leading) are the children of God. Rom. 8:14.

Gal. 5:16 reads, "Walk in the Spirit and you will not fulfil the lust of the flesh." He makes it possible for one to resist the flesh. If Christ our Model, when He was in this world, needed the Holy Spirit before He started His ministry, one can understand how indispensable the Holy Spirit is in a believer's life. He is the one who will minister the truth of the Word and His fruits inside man. Gal. 5:22-23. The purpose is to reproduce the life of Christ in man as He glorifies Christ. When Jesus entered the Synagogue, He was given the book of Isaiah to read. When He opened it, He read from Isa. 61:1.

"The Spirit of the Lord is upon Me; to preach good tidings to the meek. He hath sent me to bind the broken hearted; to proclaim liberty to the captives and the opening of the prison to them that are bound." Jesus was spirit filled and spirit led. This fact was also confirmed at His baptism. He was empowered for ministry. When we are spirit filled, we are supposed to speak in the tongue of the Spirit, be obedient to His leading, and walk in His fruits. The function of the Holy Spirit covers every need of man. Only Christ can baptise in the Holy Spirit, and this comes by faith. Gal. 3:15. The Spirit of Christ in us will reflect the life of Christ in the way we think, speak or live.

As you read this book, take steps to invite Him into your life through prayers, if you have not done so already. First repent of your sins and ask for forgiveness. Be baptised in the water and pray for His indwelling. Be part of the Church, the Spiritual Body of Christ, and learn of Him. Any blasphemy against the Holy Spirit is considered unforgivable. It is written in Isa. 63:10 that although the people were God's special people, when they blasphemed against the Holy Spirit His anger came against them. God is still kind, loving and merciful, forgiving iniquity and transgression. Num.14:18. transgression. Num.14:18.

Chapter Fifteen

— SCRIPTURAL NEGLIGENCE —

"And ye shall know the truth, and the truth shall set you free." Jon. 8:32

Overconfidence: This contributes to our inability to get to the end of our destination successfully. The fact that Satan knows that no weapon fashioned against believers shall prosper does not stop him from attacking them. 1 Cor. 10:12 cautions on the need to take heed when doing well, lest one falls unconsciously. Sometimes people feel that they are almost fulfilling most of the requirements of the Kingdom. At this stage, it is necessary to do a spiritual check-up of successes and failures in order to determine the areas that need strengthening.

The scriptures reveal that some Israelites, kings, priests, prophets, etc., for some reasons, got backslidden. Some pulled themselves out through repentance and remission of those sins, while others were finally defeated by that fall. The way one responds to problems will determine the person's destiny, whether it is condemnation or justification. The case of the prophet of Judah was a pathetic historical example for all ministers of God. 1 Kings 13:20-23. He was courageous, confident, and obeyed the instructions of God carefully before his mistake. On his way home he was diverted into disobedience. It is a heart-rending mistake which God rightly used to teach future ministers and prophets a lesson. 2 Sam. 11-12.

God's Words are Yea and Amen. 2 Cor. 1:20. When in doubt humbly ask again. Gideon did so. Judg. 6:16-17. Hezekiah also asked for clarification, 2 Kings 20:9-11. Moreover repentance, which is a sign of acknowledging our sins is a powerful remedy at all times. Ps. 51:5 reminds us that in sin did our mothers conceive us and that we were shaped in iniquity. What matters to God is immediate repentance and change, which is perceived in a changed behaviour. Ps. 51:17 reads, "The sacrifices of God are a broken spirit. A broken and a contrite heart; these O God You will not despise."

Lack Of Continuity: Lack of continuity leads to outright failure or low standard performance. It has a lot to do with lack of perseverance. In Rev. 3:10 Jesus said, "Because thou hast kept the Word of My patience I also will keep thee from the hour of temptation which shall come upon all the world, to try them that dwell on the earth." This is a promise to protect those who persevere to the end. It has been said often that continuity brings freedom.

Paul in Rom. 11:22 advised the Gentile believers that they should continue in the goodness of God, otherwise they would be cut off like some of those who fell on the way. He also reminded them of the fact that if those who fell on the way repented genuinely and continued in faith, they would be reconciled back to God. So, it is today. It is the continuity of the goodness of God in one's life that will take one to Heaven. That is why it is advisable to start the walk early so that good habits can be formed and maintained earlier in life.

Jesus in Lk. 22:28 said to His disciples, "Ye are they which have continued with Me in My temptations. And I appoint unto you a kingdom as My Father has appointed unto Me. That ye may eat and drink at My table, in My Kingdom, and sit on thrones judging the twelve tribes of Israel."

No one who continues in the way of Christ will lose out in the end. In Acts 14:22 Paul encouraged the new converts to continue in faith despite the temptations and trials that arise as a result of the walk to the Kingdom.

In Jon. 8:31, Jesus said to the Jewish believers, "If ye continue in my Word, then are ye My disciples indeed." They would be guaranteed freedom from sin. When He asked His disciples to continue in His love, He meant that His type of divine love should be extended to all relationships, not only to relatives and friends.

In Rom. 2:7, Paul taught that those who continue in well doing will eventually have eternal life. In 1 Tim. 4:16, he advised Timothy to continue his pattern of sound doctrine. He noticed that some believers were being influenced by the false doctrine of the anti-Christ.

Lack of Initiative: This is usually as a result of a lack of strong faith and fear of the unknown. Faith boosts the incentive and the courage to move ahead. The centurion in Matt. 8:5-13 whose servant was paralysed took the initiative to make Jesus aware that He believed that through His spoken Word alone, his servant could be healed, because he was not worthy to have Him enter his house. Jesus was highly impressed and released healing immediately. The woman with the issue of blood, who realised that only faith could save her, took the initiative and embarked on her difficult journey to go and stealthily receive her own healing by touching the hem of Jesus's garment. She was even crawling on the ground amidst the stampede of a large crowd. Jesus confirmed that that faith had made her whole. Matt. 9:20-22. Taking the initiative is living one's faith.

In Matt. 9:2, if the men who carried the paralytic man had not taken the initiative to lower him through the roof to the ground where Jesus was preaching, he might not have been healed. If the Phoenician woman in Matt. 15:27 did not take the initiative to put forward the fact that even the dogs eat of the crumbs that fall from the master's table, her daughter might not have been healed immediately. She appealed to the compassionate, humble nature of Christ. If blind Bartimaeus in Mk. 10:52 had not decided to cry out even louder to Jesus, at the expense of ignoring all those shouting at him to keep quiet, he might not have received his healing on that day.

If Zacchaeus in Lk. 19:1-10 had not climbed to the top of the sycamore tree to try and have a glimpse of Jesus, he and his household might not have received salvation. Fear and lack of faith inhibit initiative. An opportunity lost may not be easy to come by again. It can be likened to prayers. If you do not take the initiative to always present your requests to God properly, you may be losing a lot of opportunities and blessings without realising this.

Chapter Sixteen

— IS THERE COMPROMISE?—

"My grace is sufficient for thee; for My strength is made perfect in weakness." 2 Cor.12:9

This chapter comes as a reminder of what is often taken for granted. A compromise situation is one that makes concessions and deviations from the original standard. It can be positive or negative. A scriptural compromise makes the Word of God unscriptural and negative. Repentance is perceived as a positive move while unrepentance is considered a negative compromise.

It is a common practice for man to resort to more convenient ways of dealing with problems. Exceptions are made because of many reasons, some of which will be discussed. Maybe there are vested interests to be pleased. Sometimes issues dealing with sex, money, welfare, race, etc. are compromised. Decisions of authority, after being taken, are reversed because of vested interests. Faith is then compromised.

Some General Areas of Compromise

The Word: Jesus preached one gospel, which He handed over to the Church when He was leaving this earth. This is the gospel which the Holy Spirit is spreading today through the Church. It does not call for modifications or change because every spoken word is the inspired Word of God, and His Word is yea and amen to His glory through us. 2 Cor. 1:20. Jesus not only preached one gospel but lived it perfectly because He is the Living Word. Jon. 1:1. In trying to illustrate a point in the Word, additions can unconsciously be added.

One has to be careful in order not to risk the consequences of this mistake. Rev. 22:18. A divine voice recently said to me, "Speak to them the way Jesus spoke to them. Look at what you are reading." Jer. 23:28. I am always happy to hear words of corrections, because they awaken my consciousness. Matt. 7:15 warns of false prophets and teachers whose purposes are perverted. They will be recognised by their words and teachings. These false teachers are making it difficult for people to get there. In Matt. 5:37 Jesus said, "But let your communication be yea yea, nay nay; for whatsoever is more than this cometh of evil." Believers should be careful with any teaching that is not confirmed by the Word of God. In Jon. 12:48 Jesus said, "He that rejected Me and receiveth not My Words hath one that judgeth him; The Word that I have spoken, shall judge him in the last day." The Word is a divine judge. I have come to the realisation that any deviation from the Word is like cutting off a part of Christ's body. This is not to say that I am a good doer of the Word. We are all striving.

Repentance: Repentance is an act of positive compromise and the first step towards salvation. Genuine repentance, at the appropriate time, can make God reverse His decision to punish an offender who is also able to forgive others. This goes with the remission of sins.

If that enemy who stole from you and also brought infirmity into your life genuinely repents, he can be forgiven. If you whom he hurt continues in unforgiveness, you risk the condemnation of God. All sins are against God. Without repentance and remission of sins the whole world like Sodom and Gomorrah will perish in its sins. Jesus secured repentance for all through His blood. It is a gift of grace offered to all. Everybody may eventually repent and acknowledge Jesus as Lord. The crucial issue is the timing. Some have already repented and more will. Some may be compelled to do so by the fact that they are about to die; some on the day of judgement, and others when the reality of Hell dawns. May God have mercy on us all. Isa. 1:18 reads, "Come now and let us reason together saith the Lord; Though your sins be as scarlet they shall be as white as snow. Though they be red like crimson, they shall be as wool. If ye be willing and obedient ye shall eat the good of the land. But if you refuse and rebel ye shall be devoured by the sword. For the mouth of the Lord hath spoken it."

The Almighty God in His infinite humility and love has asked us to come to Him through His Son Jesus Christ and in prayers in order to exchange dialogue on how He could get us out of sin and position us on the right way to the Kingdom. Humility, willingness and obedience on our part are key factors that will enable genuine repentance. In Ez. 18:31, God issued a warning, "Cast away from you all your transgressions whereby ye have transgressed and make ye a new heart and a new spirit. For why will ye die O house of Israel?" All He is asking for is that spirit of genuine repentance that will justify His forgiveness, so that He can put away death from His people.

Disobedience Towards the Call: You are called by the Lord and He has already reminded you of this several times. You keep giving one excuse or the other. One reason being that you prefer to be one of the generous givers, rather than a liability in the Church. You convince yourself that since you have not refused you are not in any serious sin. It is a serious case of compromise and also considered an act of lack of faith. You tend to forget that timing belongs to the Lord, not to man. This happened to me. I was trying to compromise His will and timing for my convenience. He had said to me: "I called you. I called you. I called you."

Many are called but few are chosen. I did not respond immediately because I had not come to a full realisation of what is required of a believer. I tried to postpone the time, forgetting the fact that the command came from the One Who created time and can terminate it in any life. Suddenly I noticed that all opportunities open to the work I was doing were gradually being shut, some at the point of great breakthroughs. I was then managing my late husband's company. It was obvious that something was happening because all contracts assumed the same negative pattern. After three years I went into full-time service for the Lord. Matt. 6:33 reads, "But seek first the Kingdom of God and His righteousness and all these things shall be added to you." Allow Him to bless you in due time. If you are working against the will of God for your life, pray for a direction from Him.

The Human Body: The human body belongs to God and is a tabernacle to be kept holy and not to be defiled. This is why it is called the temple of God. 1 Cor. 3:16-17 reads, "Know ye not that ye are the temple of God, and that the spirit of God dwelleth in you? If anyone defiles the temple of God, him shall God destroy, for the temple of God is holy, which temple ye are." 1 Cor. 6:18-20 reads, "Flee fornication. Every sin that a man doeth is without the body, but he that commits fornication sins against his own body." Sexual activity is scripturally allowed by God only within the boundaries of marriage; its door is a snare which should not be opened experimentally. The blood of ransom has made believers the property of God. Ps. 24:1 also affirms that "This whole earth belongs to God; the world and all who dwell there." We are all the property of the Almighty God Who created us originally in His own image. Gen. 1:26. Compromise starts from the heart where evil is conceived. The scripture says that with the heart we believe unto righteousness. Matt. 12:34 states, "For out of the abundance of the heart the mouth speaks." What proceeds from the mouth comes from the heart, which provides the arena for evil plans. If the thoughts that are good and based on the Word suddenly change and become negative, a compromise has been introduced in the heart. There is a great need to keep the thoughts continuously pure and undefiled.

Salvation: Salvation is the greatest act of positive compromise made by God and Christ the sacrificial Lamb. He wanted to arrest an unfortunate and pathetic situation in humans. He also gave us His Holy Spirit to indwell believers. and to renew hearts. When the sin of Adam and Eve plunged mankind into damnation God did not say, forget it. I will get rid of these ones and create a new species. His reaction gave an insight into His true character. He is faithful and true in everything He does. He is able to reverse any imaginable situation, Lk. 1:36, to say the least. He is merciful, kind, forgiving iniquity and transgression. Num. 14:18.

Humility: The next greatest act of positive compromise Christ made was perceived in His selfless, humble attitude towards life. Those who rejected Him forgot that He was not a man that he should be proud. This humility, which is really His natural way of life, left Him vulnerable to human criticisms and attacks. He believed and rightly taught that evil will be defeated by good. The scripture in 2 Cor. 8:9 stated that though He was rich, he made Himself poor, so that through His forbearance we might be rich. This means that through His example we may learn how to grow in all goodness. In Matt. 11:29 Jesus said, "Take my yoke upon you and learn of me for I am gentle and lowly in spirit." Adapting to the humble character of Christ is a positive change without which our salvation becomes questionable.

Man was born and groomed in the pride of the deceiver and of the world system. One of the reasons Christ came to the world was to change this. He washed the feet of His disciples. He served the needs of the poor, the oppressed and the needy. He was the friend of sinners and forgave and converted those the society regarded as unworthy. He took over the curse of God for man and allowed Himself, the Branch of God's Righteousness, to be crucified as a sinner, so that we the sinners would be justified as sinless and live.

He wanted believers to be rich and heirs of salvation and joint heirs of the Kingdom through His grace. He wanted us to attain this through His example of love, faith and humility. He allowed Himself to be mocked, tortured and killed as a criminal, willingly and with love.

The purpose for these examples is to remind us that as humans, no one is above mistakes and that there are pitfalls at every stage of growth in faith.

Peter: The Apostle Peter was loyal to Jesus and loved Him with all his spirit, soul and body. He had very strong leadership qualities. The patient and forgiving nature of Christ was key to the growth in faith of His disciples. Some of us, especially of this generation, no matter the resources that the Lord put in us, are still not subject to correction and change.

Jeroboam: As king of Israel, he did not want his people to keep going to Jerusalem to worship. He feared that they would turn to Rehoboam, son of Solomon, who tried to kill him. In 1 Kings 11:38-39 God had promised to establish his reign if he would obey Him. In 1 Kings 12:28-29 he ignored the same God Who promised to establish his rule and "asked advice and made two calves of gold, and said to the people; it is too much for you to go up to Jerusalem. "Here are your gods O Israel which brought you up from the land of Egypt." It is only God Who can understand and explain the unpredictable nature of human deviations from the truth. This was an instance of negative compromise.

Gideon: Judges 6 to end. God reassured Gideon that He was with him by the miracles He performed in his life. He led him to destroy the altar of Baal, which his father and his people were worshipping. He gave him a miraculous victory over the battle against the Midianites. He was humble and glorified God after his victory. Judges 6:25-27; 7:15-22.

In Judges 8:23, he declined an invitation to be king and said: "I will not rule over you, neither shall my son rule over you. The Lord shall rule over you." Shortly after saying this he made an ephod of gold, and they worshipped it instead of God. This is a sharp compromise that reversed the clock back to his father's days.

Everybody compromises in different ways. As one grows in faith these compromises will begin to disappear. Every compromise that Jesus made was for good and scriptural.

Jesus made a positive compromise in the case of the Gentile woman from Sidon so that the Name of God would be glorified. Her daughter was demonised and was dying. She pleaded with Jesus to deliver her. Jesus knowing all things, first explained to her that salvation must be preached to the Jews first because of their calling. He further informed her that it was not right to take the children's food and give to the dogs. He might also be testing her faith. She answered that even the dogs eat of the crumbs that fall from the table of the children. Jesus considered this answer a manifestation of great faith and instantly healed her daughter. Matt. 15:27. This response by Christ reminds us of God's Words in Isa. 1:18, which says: "Come and let us reason together. Put forward your case for which you can be acquitted."

Chapter Seventeen

— THE CHRISTLIKE WOMAN —

"A virtuous woman is a crown to her husband." Pro. 12:4

This book cannot be concluded without the addition of a separate chapter on women. This is because their scope of responsibility is wide, and the areas they are held accountable many. Most of the time the men are at work. Sometimes this creates problems. The responsibility for raising Christian children, being submissive and obedient wives, ensuring that the home is peaceful and healthy, helping to organise the men, substituting household income where the need arises, and most importantly maintaining success in their ministries and caring for their elderly relatives largely rest on women. In some civilised cultures husbands also help in spite of their busy schedules. These different areas of responsibilities, if not properly handled, can open doorways for satanic attacks that can seriously hinder the journey to the

Kingdom. This chapter will try to offer a way of getting through these responsibilities in the discussion of the Christlike woman, and the peculiar characteristics of women. It will also highlight some characteristics of women that need to be directed away from problem areas into productive activities.

The Different Characteristics of Women
Emotional
Talkative
Jealous
Compassionate
Complacent
Tendency to always give advice
Mother Instinct

Emotional
Women are emotional in the sense that they are more reactive and easily worried about issues than their husbands. They are easily given to tears and argumentative expressions. One wonders where faith comes in here. The scripture teaches that fear, anxiety and anger are not of the Holy Spirit, and can lead to hasty and unhealthy decisions. These need to be replaced by faith, love, peace, joy and a genuine fear of God. Situations in the family that can give rise to panic include ill health, financial problems, threat

to one's job, an unstable marriage and the realisation that one has ignored the ministry. The female singles looking forward to marrying a good husband live in fear and panic as the years go by. This leads to hasty mistakes of fornication, an unscriptural lifestyle entered into in order to keep a man. The scripture in Rom. 9:16 makes one to understand that it is not of him that willeth, nor of him that runneth, but of God that showeth mercy." Neither fornication, nor all those artificial things designed to attract attention can guarantee a man's character in a life. It is only the Holy Spirit Who can do this, and this is by the grace of God. Zech. 4:6. All these explosive situations can only be put right by exercising faith and waiting on God to order it the way He planned.

The fact that women are more emotional than men make them more compassionate and able to feel and articulate people's suffering and needs. This is why they are easily given to tears. It is scriptural to feel and fulfil the needs of others. Gal. 6:2.

Talkative
This tendency often leads to some women gossiping and some nagging their husbands. This attitude is often continued in large, crowded churches where some may be talking to their children. This may have informed Paul's

statement in 1 Cor. 14:34 that women should keep quiet in the Church. He was not discriminatory, because in Gal. 3:28 he said, "There is neither Jew nor Greek, there is neither slave nor free; there is neither male nor female" He concluded by saying, "for you are all one in Christ Jesus."

Pro. 31:26 states that a godly woman speaks with wisdom and the fear of God. Excessive flow of words creates problems in marriage. James 3:6 teaches that "the tongue is a fire, a world of iniquity." If this habit is unchecked, it can bring great discomfort and unrest to others. A woman that does not exercise discretion in all that she says can unconsciously expose her husband's plans and secrets.

Jealousy
This can be as a result of lack of trust in a husband. It can lead to an attitude of over-possessiveness and false accusations. This weakness can distract the mind from the things of God. While the godly woman is busy doing the will of God as a helper and living holy, the Lord will not allow any stranger to evade her marriage.

Advice Giving
There is nothing wrong in a wife giving good and worthwhile advice to her husband. This is biblical. Sarah advised Abraham to send away the bond woman Hagar and her son from the house because Ishmael was being

nasty to Isaac. Abraham wanted to reject this advice because Ishmael too was his son. In Gen. 21:12, God said to Abraham, "Let it not be grievous in thy sight because of the lad and because of thy bondwoman. In all that Sarah hath said unto thee, harken unto her voice, for in Isaac shall thy seed be called." When a believing husband receives advice and observes that it is always substantiated by the scriptures, he will always accept it. If it is always based on worldly trends, he will always question such. Abraham was one person who showed a steadfast endurance and an unwavering faith in all the tests that God put before him. It is not easy to collect your own child and just cast him away with his mother with very scanty provision in the forest. Serious problems can also arise when the role of the wife is shifted from that of a helper to that of a decision maker. This is unscriptural. All advice should be based on the scriptures.

Good Women and Mistaken Wrong Advice

The purpose for writing this is to inform ourselves of how easy it is to make a mistake when the mind strays away from the Word and is emotionally stressed.

Saul's daughter Michal, who was David's wife, tried to impose an unscriptural view on David, but he rejected it. 2 Sam. 6:16-23. She felt that he was too big to dance for the Lord before the people. She suffered the consequence of that advice. A single piece of wrong advice can easily hinder human destiny. Pro. 31:11 taught that the virtuous woman was the heart and trust of her husband because her advice did him good.

Job's Wife: She was more distressed than her husband over his suffering, and was only trying to contain the situation. She needed to say something urgently. Job 2:9. He ignored it. Under such strange situations it is always advisable to keep quiet and go to God in prayers. She later regretted this advice. Job 42:12-13.

Sarah: Being very zealous that the will of God should not be delayed, and since it would appear as if her body was delaying, she advised her husband to go ahead and have the promised child through Hagar, her maid. She later regretted this advice. One cannot set the time for God, Who created time and controls it.

Rebekah: She advanced from the level of an adviser to that of a planner and a decision maker. Gen. 27:5-13. She misadvised Jacob her son, and deceived Isaac her husband. Maybe the emotional nature of women has a lot to do with this. Like Sarah she went ahead of God to implement His prophecy, which said: "And the older shall serve the younger." Gen. 25:23b. God has His timing and method.

Complacency

In Pro. 31:23 the godly woman was the weaker sex, but we are also told that she had physical and mental strength. These qualities were also responsible for her success as a wife and worker in the vineyard of God. In Isa. 32:9-11 God is talking to all the women who are idle and not hardworking and have abandoned their jobs and ministry. Although the responsibility of being a wife, mother, etc. is not easy, God would like these to be up and doing, especially in their ministries.

Children and Parents

Children are supposed to look after old parents, widows and in-laws. Sometimes when children are grown, in trying to fulfil this obligation, problems arise. There are believing parents who have reported irresponsibility on the part of their children. There are also some believers who have reported that their unbelieving parents are unduly trying to rearrange their lives for them and change their faith. 2 Kings 21:6. Some parents have also complained that their children are aloof and apathetic.

In Matt. 10:36 Jesus said, "A man's enemies will be those of his own household." If there is a threat of initiation, it becomes necessary to maintain a scriptural, healthy distance while interceding for them and most importantly praying for God's protection on your life. If you can lead them to Christ, that would be the greatest honour you can bestow on them. God in the book of Ezekiel 18:20 said, "The son shall not bear the guilt of the father nor the father bear the guilt of the son. The righteousness of the righteous shall be upon himself, and the wickedness of the wicked shall be upon himself." There are still today a few Abrahamic cases where God has asked the individuals to move away from an evil parental foundation that is trying to engulf them. God is the same yesterday, today and forever.

What God Disapproves of

Isa. 3:16 reveals some of the things that God hates about some women. Among these are haughtiness and pride. In Pro. 6:17-19 pride is listed as one of the seven things which God hates. Another thing God hates in women is the habit of walking with stretched forth necks. This means displaying their necks for all to see. This is the sin of bodily exposure, which is common today. Another is walking with wanton eyes, which is all about immorality and idleness. In the book of Isa. 32:9-11 women are advised to keep away from these habits so that they do not risk the condemnation of God.

Time Spent in the Ministry

Patterns of behaviour among women can differ in different

countries. This can be as a result of differences and changes in cultural influences. In Africa mothers no longer remain at home in order to mind their young ones. It is now common to have a professional resident house help and women prefer to work in order to complement household income or to build up a career for themselves. In some European countries childcare subsidies are provided. Working or staying at home, is a matter of agreement between the husband and the wife. Often this decision is made long before marriage. Some may decide to stay at home until the children are of school age. Women should pray to God for wisdom and guidance on how to accommodate the work of ministry in their lives. Hopefully as the children grow older, more time will be devoted to this demand. We as women are to allow the grace of God to be perceived in the way we discharge our responsibilities as wives, mothers, singles and workers. Today women who are willing and available are called to discharge any responsibility in the body of Christ.

Jesus recognised and appreciated the role of women in His ministry, although He had no woman among the first twelve disciples. But when the number of the disciples expanded, He had women followers. In Acts 1:14 among the 120 whom Jesus asked to go to the upper room and continue in prayers and await the outpouring of the Holy

Spirit, women were there. Joel 2:28-29 reads, "And it shall come to pass afterwards that I will pour out My Spirit upon all flesh; and your sons and daughters shall prophesy, your old men shall dream dreams, your young men shall see visions. And also upon My men servants and maid servants in those days will I pour out my spirit." Both men and women were given the opportunity to receive and operate in the Spirit. Phoebe was a deacon. Rom. 16:1. In Rom. 16:3-5 Priscilla and Aquila had a church in their house. In the book of Phil. 4:3, Paul entreated the Philippian Church to assist those women who laboured with him in the gospel. Women spoke, preached and prophesied in the early Church.

Jesus showed divine compassion towards the problems attendant in the lives of some women and used it to draw some of them into the ministry. An example was the woman they brought to Him taken in adultery. He did not condemn her but ministered repentance and remission of sins to her. Jon. 8:10-11. In the case of the woman who anointed his feet, He made no reference to her sins but blessed her for anointing Him in preparation for His death. Lk. 7:44-45. She genuinely repented and became one of His followers. The Samaritan woman He met at the pool who had had five husbands He converted to an evangelist. Such women, as a result of the way that their problems were handled, repented immediately and glorified God. In Lk. 10:39-42

Mary appreciated what Christ was saying, and sat at His feet to hear and learn more. Martha received a correction from Jesus because her mind was bothered by a lot of things she wrongly valued, and as a result she missed the Word of life that Jesus was teaching. When Jesus corrected Martha, He was indirectly asking all the women burdened with problems to come to Him the Living Word in faith and receive rest from their problems. Do we, like Mary, have our priorities right? How do we apportion our time to our different responsibilities as wives, mothers, singles, workers and ministers in the vineyard of God? How do we reflect the Word in our lives?

Christ is the solution to all the problems in life. All mothers have to be prayer addicts at this time of moral decay. There is an urgent need to commit all the problems of the family to God in prayers as often as possible every day. The Spirit of the Lord has a way of revealing to each the right way of getting things done. As a parent God has entrusted His heritage into your hands as your children in order to bring them up in the ways of Christ, in order to produce His likeness. Ps. 127:3. Continuous prayers should be made for children who have not received Christ as their Saviour. Pray that their hearts will be fertile to receive the Word, and that the spirit of unbelief will be uprooted from their hearts. As a believer the Holy Spirit will reveal to you areas of impending problems that you need to commit to God in prayers. Do not cease to plead the blood of Jesus in their hearts. Pray also that the Holy Spirit will minister the Spirit of repentance to them. 1 Tim. 2:4 states that God desires that all men should be saved and come to the knowledge of the truth. Acts 16:31 reads, "Believe in the Lord Jesus Christ, and you will be saved you and your household."

I was once invited to pray for a baby during her dedication service. A divine voice said, "Pray for the parents." As I was wondering who needed the prayers, the child or the parents, the truth of that command immediately came to me. The Lord has said it all. It is the parents that will bring up the child in the ways of the Lord since children are a heritage of the Lord. They therefore need serious prayers in order to carry out this assignment. Matt. 18:6 states that if anyone misleads any of the little ones, it would be better for them if a millstone were put around their necks and they were cast into the depths of the sea. Parents need prayers to receive the knowledge, wisdom and understanding from God. Prayers should also be made for their spiritual, mental and physical empowerment, and for continuous guidance. These children, although under the protection of God, can pick up habits from their parents as they grow.

Women and Submission

Women are created helpers to their husbands. Gen. 2:18. They are accountable to God on how well this role is played. Husbands are supposed to show appreciation for this. There are some instances where the income of the woman far exceeds that of her husband. There are also some cases where the woman is the only bread winner. Through the cooperation of both, and a humble enduring attitude based on love, this situation will be a joyful one. The wife will still be subject to her husband in spite of her financial strength. In a situation where the husband is the bread winner and is overtly male conscious, the wife should commit everything to God in prayers.

Sarah obeyed Abraham and called him Lord. 1 Pet. 3:6. The role of a helper is perceived in the Christian world as a noble one. Jesus made Himself the bondservant of man, which is lower than a helper. Submission, although peculiar to some women these days, should be regarded as mutual by both husbands and wives. Eph. 5:21 reads, "Submitting yourselves one to another in the fear of God." In situations where the husbands are not believers the principle of submission still obtains. 1 Pet. 3:1 reads, "Be submissive to your own husbands that even if any did not obey the Word, they without a Word may be won by the conduct of their wives." If the husband compels her to disobey the Word, she can bring the matter to the Church for the right scriptural advice.

In some cultures, the married woman finds that the life of service is central to her responsibility. This is because she has to serve her immediate family, extended family members, the elderly, friends, organisations, groups that come to the house, and those who solicit for help whenever the need arises. In some cultures, the burden is shared between the husband and wife. A godly woman is a joyful and privileged person because in her life of service she is obeying the Word of God.

The Word of God should inform parents' attitude and the upbringing of the children on a regular basis. This responsibility demands that parents know the Word themselves very well. In Deut. 6:6-9 God instructed the Israelites to this effect. "And these Words which I command thee this day, shall be in thine heart. And thou shalt teach them diligently unto thine children. And shall talk of them when thou sittest in thy house, and when thou walkest by the way, and when thou liest down, and when thou risest up, and thou shalt bind them for a sign upon thine hand, and they shalt be as frontlets between thine eyes. And thou shalt write them upon the posts of thine house, and on the gates, write them on the doorposts of your house, and on your gates." It is also faster and easier to teach children by living the Word yourself because their ever-watchful eyes are always ready to copy anything they observe. They should be taught how to study the scriptures regularly.

Try to correct your children by quoting the Bible to them regularly. They will also learn to memorise them. It is very important to explain to the children the things that attract punishment from God and the ones that will earn His praises. Give them examples of your earlier encounters with Him. Use the Israelites to teach them God's love, mercy and continuous forgiveness for His children. His promises to those who are obedient, and His punishment towards those who in spite of His continuous warnings and patience have continued in sin; that salvation is only for those who believe in the victory at the Cross and forsake sin.

Some Exceptionally, Scriptural Women

Mary, The Mother Of Christ
Sarah, Abraham's Wife
Hannah
The Virtuous Woman

Mary, The Mother of Jesus

Mary suddenly found herself chosen to carry part of the burden of the world. God, Who foresees the end from the beginning, and Whose judgements are true and righteous altogether, has judged and empowered her to carry this burden victoriously. When the reality of what will happen to her was explained to her by the angel, she neither raised any arguments against nor refused it. All she asked was how the incarnation will take place, given her situation as being betrothed to Joseph. She realised that from a human perspective she stood a chance of not only losing her impending marriage but being stigmatised and branded a fornicator who might even not have a husband after that. She also had to confront Joseph and her parents.

She acted bravely without fear because of her unwavering faith in God. It showed a remarkable example of one who, convinced that the instruction came from God, could take an individual stance despite all oppositions. She was prepared to suffer for the rest of her life for what she did not do in order to please God. Mary was brave, trusting, willing, loyal and understanding like a child. Jesus was born in a manger. Before the three wise men came with their gifts, she was content with the below-the-poverty-line type of life. This is because she set her mind on things above and not on things below. She was sacrificial and enduring. Simeon prophesied in Lk. 2:34 that a sword would pierce through Mary's soul. She lived with this thought in her mind until the day of Christ's crucifixion, when it happened. She stood firm by her Son until His last minute on the Cross. She was the ideal Christian mother and wife.

Sarah, Abraham's Wife
She was a devoted, humble and obedient wife, who had come to terms with her own cross of barrenness. She did not know that God had His own special plans pertaining to

her. After God's promises, like her husband, she eventually believed and developed faith, although she was eighty-six years old. She was obedient to the point of not arguing when her husband asked her to tell Pharoah that she was his sister. Gen. 12:20. She called her husband Lord.

Hannah

1 Sam. 1:28; 2:1-10. In Hannah we see faith, steadfast endurance, persistence, discipline and politeness. She followed her husband every year to Shiloh to present her request of the blessing of her womb to God. She had the faith that she would eventually be a mother of children. It can be seen from this case how God answers the prayers of His children who persist without giving up or sliding into sin. She made a vow to hand over the child to God and immediately she weaned the child she did so. Some women have found themselves forced by desperation to make such vows and have discovered that the fulfilment was not that easy. Somebody who made such a vow said that she was waiting for the right place and a trustworthy pastor and yet the child continued to grow. It is a frightful decision that requires full-scale planning before such a request is submitted. Eccl. 5:4-5 reads: "When you make a vow to God do not delay to pay it; pay what you vowed; for He has no pleasure in fools. Pay what you have vowed. Better not to vow than to vow and not pay."

Chapter Eighteen

— THE REWARDS OF THE KINGDOM —

"But as it is written, Eye hath not seen, nor ear heard, neither have entered into the heart of man, the things which God hath prepared for them that love Him." 1 Cor. 2:9

We have discussed some of the ways of getting to the Kingdom and the hurdles that one needed to go through before getting there. The rewards of the Kingdom are many and far exceed anyone's imagination. Rewards act as an encouragement to both the believers and unbelievers. They is a continuous reminder in the Scripture, in Heb. 12:2 which read, "...looking unto Jesus, the author and finisher of our faith; Who for the joy that was set before Him, endured the cross, despised the shame; and has sat down at the right hand of the throne of God." The reward can be perceived as two-folds: the ones experienced on this earth, and the ones to be experienced in Heaven. This chapter acts as an encouragement for obedience to the Word. We are to focus on these rewards like Jesus and labour tirelessly by grace for the Kingdom of God.

"Rom. 8:18-19 reads, "For I reckon that the sufferings of this present time are not worthy to be compared with the glory which shall be revealed in us."

The Lord rewards according to one's input into the Kingdom. If you think you have put in so much into the Kingdom, but did not do so willingly or with love, and humility, there may still be some scriptures that need to be obeyed. 1 Cor. 13:3-5 reads, "And though I bestow all my goods to feed the poor, and though I give my body to be burnt, but have not love, it profiteth me nothing. Love suffers long and is kind, love does not envy, love does not parade itself, is not puffed up, does not behave rudely, does not seek its own, is not provoked, thinks no evil." Love testifies that you are in the right relationship with God, because God is love. Christ gave His Life willingly and out of love. In apportioning rewards, God's judgements are neither unfair nor partial, but true and righteous altogether. Rev. 19:11.

1 Pet. 1:17 reads, "And if ye call on the Father Who without respect of persons judgeth according to every man's work, pass the time of your sojourning here in fear." Many years

past my spiritual eyes were opened to see somebody like a divine judge sitting down and people were coming to receive either instructions or something from his hand while others were reporting back. I was just standing there idly, observing everything. Suddenly the divine figure turned and said to me, "Felicia, people like you" and he flung his right hand as far back as it could go. I was seriously alarmed. If according to Rev. 3:16 those who were lukewarm would be spewed out, what will happen to those who were idle? What he meant was that if I was not up and doing like the others, he would cast me backwards far away from his presence. "He who has ears to hear, let him hear." What we put into the Kingdom is what we get, be it faith, time, love, hard work, patience, thought, care, etc.

The parable of the talents in Matt. 25:14-29 is a good example of how rewards will be apportioned. The point being emphasised is the faithful discharge of one's duties in the body of Christ. The efforts of two servants bore fruits, but the third, who was idle, just making sure that he did not violate his interpretation of people's principles, reproduced nothing. As a result he lost what was originally given to him.

A willing and obedient attitude of mind attracts a lot of rewards, both on earth and in Heaven. On earth these rewards can include everlasting after life, righteousness, joy, deliverance, spiritual growth, healing, protection, provision etc. In Heaven it can be everlasting life, a new body, name, a crown, peace, joy, fellowship with the Lord, permanent security, divine service and an accommodation. From the information we can get from the Scriptures, especially the book of Revelation, one can say that in Heaven the perfection of beauty in everything God created is beyond human comprehension. This testifies that God is the Father and Creator of beauty, perfection and artistic design. Everything is beautifully, intricately and purposefully made to radiate the perfection of the Creator. Praise God. Ps. 139:14 says, "I will praise You, for I am fearfully and wonderfully made." This perfection is supposed to radiate in the lives of genuine believers.

It is written that "God is not unjust to forget thine work and labour of love which ye have shown towards His Name; in that ye have ministered to the saints and do minister." The reward of eternal rest is assured those who live a holy life and die in the Lord. Rev. 14:13, God's rewards also cover the area of man's generosity, humble service, kindness, love, suffering and enduring willingly on behalf of Christ, tithing and offerings, praying for those who hate you and despitefully use you, hard work, etc.

Rev. 21:4 reads, "And God shall wipe away all tears from their eyes; and there shall be no more death, nor sorrow nor crying. Neither shall there be any more pain, for the former things are passed away." God's presence will not allow any feeling of sorrow.

Rev. 2:7 reads, "He that hath an ear let him hear what the spirit says to the Churches. To him that overcometh will I give to eat of the Tree of Life, which is in the midst of the Paradise of God." The tree of Life is the spiritual food that will sustain eternal life.

Rev. 7:9 says, "After this I beheld and lo, a great multitude which no man could number, of all nations, and kindreds, peoples, and tongues, stood before the throne and before the Lamb, clothed with white robes, and palms in their hands." These are the redeemed of all historical groups, the white robes and palms symbolising righteousness and victory. These are only a few of the many scriptures that reveal heavenly reward.

These rewards are conditional and based on the keeping of the words of the scriptures. This is because He is a perfect God Who does not want any imperfection in His Kingdom. His blessings are also immense, perfect and unimaginable.

Conditions for Claiming Rewards

In Matt. 5:17 Jesus warned that He did not come to destroy the existing laws and the prophets but to fulfil them. "For verily I say unto you, till heaven and earth pass, one jot or one title shall in no wise pass from the law, till all be fulfilled." This stresses the need to fulfil all the commandments but by grace and through faith in the Lord Jesus Christ.

Deut. 5:29 reads, "O that there were such a heart in them, that they would fear me, and keep all my Commandments always, and Statutes, that it might be well with them and their children for ever." Obedience and the fear of God are required. There is an emphasis on the words "always" and "all". These seem to be the conditions that will guarantee the reward. It may sound difficult, but we know that with the God we serve, all things are possible. The idea of obeying all the commandments has been eased off by the death and resurrection of Christ, which expects us to live through Him as if all those sins are forever dead.

There are some psalms that deal specifically with God's blessings on this earth. Psalm 128 talks of the rewards of righteousness. It has over eight blessings for those who will continue to live in the fear of God and in His ways.

Psalm 34 has a scriptural compilation of the rewards of a righteous man on this earth. The book of Deut. 28 also has a compilation of the blessings of God for those who are obedient and walking with God.

Ps. 128 is a psalm of righteousness which has over seven blessings of God pronounced on those who will continue to live in fear of Him and in His ways.

Psalm 1 is called the Psalm of Righteousness. All the blessings here are for those who keep away from sinful thoughts, actions and friends. They are not scornful but humble and read and study the Word regularly. The following blessings will overtake them. They will be positioned for growth. God will sustain and protect them. Their fruitfulness will be assured.

They shall not suffer loss.

They will experience all-round prosperity.

God will continue to enable them to sustain their righteous ways.

It can be seen that God's blessings are reciprocal. There is something God wants from us in return for His blessings. We have to qualify for them by faith in Jesus in order to receive His grace. In the Old Testament the following scriptures testify to this fact of reciprocity.

Ps. 91:1: "He that dwelleth in the secret place of the Most High, shall abide under the Shadow of the Almighty." These are those who do His Will.

Ps. 91:14: "Because he has set his love upon Me therefore will I deliver him. I will set him on high because he knows my Name." To love God is to receive from Him.

Ps. 27:4-5: "One thing have I desired of the Lord, that will I seek after; that I may dwell in the house of the Lord all the days of my life; to behold the beauty of the Lord and to enquire in His Temple. For in the time of trouble He shall hide me in His pavilion; in the secret of His tabernacle shall He hide me. He shall set me up upon a rock." The psalmist's wish had to be fulfilled in practical obedience.

In the book of Gal. 3:13-14, Christ suffered excruciatingly in order that we may receive not only everlasting life but the blessings of our father Abraham through His Seed Jesus, and the promise of the Holy Spirit through faith in the Same Jesus. He bore the pain and the penalty for our sins. We are required to endure just the inconvenience of the denial of every single one of those sins.

Lk. 18:29 reads, "Assuredly I say to you, there is no one who has left house or parents or brothers or wife or children for the sake of the Kingdom of God, who shall not receive many times more in this present time, and in the age to come, eternal life."

We all know that by strength shall no one be able to make the Kingdom.1 Sam. 2:9; Zech. 4:6. This can only be done by obeying the call of Jesus in the book of Jon. 3:5, in order to receive the power of the Holy Spirit, Who will make this possible. It reads, " Jesus answered, "Most assuredly I say to you, unless one is born of water and the Spirit he cannot enter the Kingdom of God. " This means being identified with Jesus death and resurrection. Only He can baptise with the Holy Spirit and with fire.

Chapter Nineteen

— THE SELF-IMPOSED CURSE —

"And whoso breaketh an hedge, a serpent shall bite him." Eccl. 10:8

It has been observed that people hardly pronounce curses these days, because of the teachings in the scriptures and a greater awareness of the implications of such unfortunate pronouncements. It would also appear as if the actions and behaviours of some people at this end time, open the doorways for the spirits attendant to particular curses to walk into their lives. 2 Tim. 3: 1-7; Zech. 5:4 reads, "I will send out the curse says the Lord of hosts. It shall enter the house of the thief and the house of the one who swears falsely by My Name. It shall remain in the midst of his house; and consume it with its timber and stones." Sin, infirmity, sicknesses and diseases, poverty, early death, barrenness, backwardness, etc. are curses. Some are self-imposed, while others are not. Curses will not make it easy for anyone to get there unless they are broken. These can be broken through strong warfare prayers and fasting. Breaking any commandment that has a punishment attached to it attracts an immediate curse. Curses frustrate the walk to the Kingdom. Pro. 26:2 reads, "Like a flitting sparrow, like a flying swallow, so a curse without cause shall not alight."

There are some whose spiritual safety are under threat and may likely lead to living under a curse. Like Abraham they need to be detached from the object of pollution and danger. Our entire purpose for living in this world is to be saved and sanctified in order to appear before God in righteousness

Chapter Twenty

— CONCLUSION —

The walk to Heaven needs to be Christlike, selfless, and sacrificial. Although Christ earned righteousness for all who would believe, one is supposed to maintain that state of righteousness as a way of life on a daily basis. This is why the apostle Paul asked in the book of Romans 6:1, "What shall we say then? Shall we continue in sin that grace may abound?"

When Jesus comes this time, He will have no time for anyone of us still living in any known sin. Such will be required to make their own sacrifices for sin with their own blood. His blood will no longer be available for that service. He is only coming for those repentant sinners whom the Holy Spirit has prepared for Him. The Holy Spirit will also not be available for the laborious task of converting and renewing man's heart. Just as Jesus resurrected, because no sin was found in Him so all who die in Him without sin will be resurrected. He said to Martha in Jon. 11:25-26, "I am the resurrection and the life. He who believes in Me though he may die, shall live. And whoever lives and believes in Me shall never die." Bodily resurrection is promised to all those who would die in Christ.

Moses was one of those closest to God, but because of a brief spontaneous manifestation of anger when he struck the rock, he lost the chance of entering the promised land before his death. He had long repented of this while he was alive and is now in Heaven. Matt. 17:1-3. Sin is opposed to the purity of God. David, the friend of God, also made a mistake and repented immediately, and is now in heaven. He too like Moses suffered sin's consequences on this earth. Paul the apostle was not an exception. Just as they repented and were forgiven, you and I need to repent today of any known sin, so that we can be forgiven. Everybody came from a background of sin and needs that special gift of repentance and remission in order to survive. Ps. 51:5. When Jesus called Peter to the discipleship, before he accepted, the first thing he said to Jesus was, "Depart from me for I am a sinful man O Lord." Lk. 5:8b. You can say that the Church is a congregation of repentant sinners. It is necessary to grasp that forgiveness now while it is still available and the blood of cleansing. since His arrival seems imminent. God is still loving, merciful and forgiving.

This book ends with the following biblical principles.

1. Success demands greater humility and service.
2. A right relationship with God is based on the blood of Jesus.
3. A boil in the body is likened to a misleading messenger of God.
4. A move towards righteousness attracts satanic opposition.
5. The new birth makes you a spiritual son, not a physical one.
6. Continued silence from God may be an indication of dissatisfaction.
7. How long will God allow you to continue in sin?
8. Without the crown of thorns, there is no crown of glory.
9. Your high expectations for yourself is like a drop of water in a river in comparison to God's for you.
10. It is not the backwardness that he focuses on but the doorway through which it came.

11. Continuity guarantees victory.

12. When you please the Lord you will get much from Him.

11. We must ignore and move ahead.

13. Secret things are to be kept secret.

14. A leader serves, not only in humility but in love.

15. Brokenness is a vital aspect of spiritual growth.

16. Self-restraint is a key to righteousness.

17. A disciplined eye is a way of righteousness.

18. The blood of Jesus is in conjunction with rigteousness.

19. Victory is to endure the pain of living righteously.

20. Certainty is never to step back into the previous mistake.

21. If your reason is not biblical, exercise great restraint.

22. Good works do not necessarily produce good characters.

23. Grace demands a denial of sinful habits.

24. It is a blessing to have God speak either good or bad to you.

25. Any time you bring a smile on the face of the Lord you are closer to fulfilling all righteousness.

26. God's reprimand is the way to correction and a place of favour before Him.

27. If you are happy, is God also happy with you?

28. If you want only good prophecies, how can you know the enemy's plans against you?

29. The quality of faith is more important than its quantity.

30. Christian leadership is selfless service.

31. A wrong choice is not different from an albatross around the neck.

32. A negative compromise is the sure way to failure.

33. Sin is an invisible divide.

34. Unrepentance is as a result of pride.

35. Immediate correction is a saving grace.

36. A leader respects and serves those he leads.

37. Brokenness gives rise to spiritual growth.

38. Do not allow the devil to steal your time.

39. Faith in Christ overrides all relationships.

40. It is better to climb securely from the ground than to fall from a slippery top.

41. Humility and self-respect move in opposite directions.

42. The Kingdom is an internal movement perceived in practical living.

43. Do not condemn yourself with your tongue.

44. All must pass through the fire, either to be purged or to be consumed.

45. Will the God of perfection accept half-hearted presentation?

46. God's criticism is the sure way to correction and change.

47. It is not who is happy with himself but whom God is happy with.

48. You want to be left alone; will God allow you to remain in a state of unrighteousness?

49. If our greatest fear is of death, why do we reject Christ's offer of everlasting life?

50. A negative compromise is the doorway to failure.

51. Immediate correction is like a saving grace.

52. Just as He hung in total surrender to pay the price of our sins, willingly endure the discomfort of denying those sins.

53. Allow your flesh to be crucified on earth and not in hell.

54. Zealousness drives away lukewarmness.

55. Pride has a stench which God cannot stand.

56. Happiness in affliction generates fast spiritual growth.

57. Physical death does not end conscious existence.

58. A simple experiment with sin is the sure way to enslavement.

59. Faith is living as if sin is dead in you.

60. A heartfelt fear of God leads to righteousness.

61. Do not use your intellect to find the narrow way.

62. Grace demands obedience to the Word of God.

63. Healing comes by the denial of the pain of giving up sin.

64. Will the God of perfection accept half-hearted presentation?

65. In life we are either moving positively or negatively.

66. Not how well we lead but how well we serve.

67. Do not give glory to man for what God has done for you.

Milton Keynes UK
Ingram Content Group UK Ltd.
UKHW020049271124
451585UK00012B/1146